MARLOWE AND
THE EARLY
SHAKESPEARE

MARLOWE AND THE EARLY SHAKESPEARE

THE CLARK LECTURES

Trinity College, Cambridge, 1951

by

F. P. WILSON

OXFORD
AT THE CLARENDON PRESS

Oxford University Press, Ely House, London W.1

GLASGOW NEW YORK TORONTO MELBOURNE WELLINGTON
CAPE TOWN SALISBURY IBADAN NAIROBI LUSAKA ADDIS ABABA
BOMBAY CALCUTTA MADRAS KARACHI LAHORE DACCA
KUALA LUMPUR HONG KONG TOKYO

FIRST EDITION 1953
REPRINTED LITHOGRAPHICALLY IN GREAT BRITAIN
AT THE UNIVERSITY PRESS, OXFORD
BY VIVIAN RIDLER, PRINTER TO THE UNIVERSITY
FROM CORRECTED SHEETS OF THE FIRST EDITION
1954, 1963, 1967

PREFACE

THE five lectures printed in this book are the Clark Lectures given at Trinity College, Cambridge, in the Lent Term of 1951. Passages have been included which there was not time to deliver, and to the last lecture a few new paragraphs have been added. While some notes and references may be found at the end of the book, the references by no means represent the sum of my indebtedness to the many who have written on my theme. Here I can only mention a general debt to Dr. F. S. Boas's *Christopher Marlowe* (1940), Professor J. Bakeless's *The Tragicall History of Christopher Marlowe* (1942), and to the editors of the standard edition of Marlowe's works published by Messrs. Methuen between 1930 and 1933. I have also to acknowledge my particular obligation to two other Marlowe scholars, Dr. Ethel Seaton and Sir Walter Greg, who have been good enough to read my manuscript.

To the Council of Trinity College, to Dr. G. M. Trevelyan, late Master, and to members of the Cambridge English Faculty, I am grateful for hospitality and many kindnesses.

F. P. W.

CONTENTS

I

INTRODUCTORY

ANYONE who speaks about Marlowe is faced
with three main problems. First, the problem
of his character. We know more about his twenty-
nine years than about Shakespeare's fifty-two years,
and for two main reasons: the one is that Marlowe
was not the 'gentle' Marlowe; the other is that he
went to a university, for universities and colleges
are pious conservers of records. Yet much that we
know about him is highly enigmatic. In a sense we
know too much about him, and too little. We *know*
we cannot write a biography of Shakespeare; we
think we can write one of Marlowe. Secondly, there
is the problem of his text. The only plays of his to
be published in his lifetime are the two parts of
Tamburlaine, for he died some years before the
habit of reading plays became widespread; and he
had no Heming and Condell to collect his plays and
do an office to the dead. Edward Blount discharged
his duty to his friend by publishing *Hero and Leander*,
but, unfortunately, did nothing for the plays. The
consequence is that the texts that have descended
to us vary from the comparative goodness of *Dido*
and *Tamburlaine* to the desperate corruption of *The*

Massacre at Paris. Thirdly, there is the problem of chronology. It is hardly an exaggeration to say that of all the plays of Marlowe and the early plays of Shakespeare the only ones which can be assigned with reasonable certainty to within a very few months of their date of composition are the two parts of *Tamburlaine.* If in these lectures I were to engage in controversy about Marlowe's character or his text or the chronology of his plays, I should have no time to speak about him and Shakespeare as dramatic poets, my main concern. On these problems I shall have to touch from time to time, but so compendiously that I may seem to be satisfied that I have travelled over Marlowe's mind and believe that the problems of text and chronology have been settled once for all. That is not so. In his life of Seth Ward, Walter Pope the astronomer tells a story of Lawrence Rooke of Eton and King's, an original member of the Royal Society:

I never knew him affirm any thing positively, that was dubious. I have said to him, Mr. Rooke, I have found out the reason of such a Phenomenon, and given him my Arguments for it, which when he had heard, he has often replied in this manner; And why may it not as well be thus, bringing his reasons for another Hypothesis. Lord, said I then to him, now you confound me, pray tell me what is your Opinion? To which his usual Answer was, *I have no opinion.*

In no circumstances could this remark have fallen from the lips of Rooke's contemporary, Sir Thomas Browne. Browne always had an opinion. While I find Browne more attractive metal, I am bound to confess that in the face of the many unsolved problems that relate to the plays of Marlowe and the early Shakespeare I often find myself in company with Lawrence Rooke.

By way of introduction let me begin by putting this question: What was the state of the English theatre in the fifteen-eighties, when Marlowe and presumably Shakespeare wrote their earliest plays? Sir Philip Sidney, writing in the earliest years of this decade, could find only one play which he could praise, and that a play already twenty years old. True, *Gorboduc* was faulty in time and place, yet it had the merits of climbing to the height of Seneca his style and of teaching delightfully notable morality. For the contemporary romantic comedy and tragi-comedy, Sidney had nothing but contempt, as also for the scurrility of the comic writers who sought to lift up a loud laughter instead of the delight proper to comedy. If we think him harsh in excepting only *Gorboduc* from general condemnation, for which plays written in the quarter of a century before 1581–3 should we plead? For *Cambyses*? Or *Sir Clyomon and Sir Clamydes*? Or *Common*

Conditions? Or *The Conflict of Conscience?* Or *The Three Ladies of London?* Sidney's misfortune as a critic was that he had no body of good contemporary drama to criticize. He was writing just before the dawn. By 1580 there was nothing in drama comparable to *The Shepheardes Calender*, for poetry had not yet spilled over into drama: so he could find nothing to praise but *Gorboduc*.

If I were asked for an opinion why the drama became poetical in the fifteen-eighties and not before, I should have to reply, 'I have no opinion': for I cannot think that the man who asks that sort of question would be fobbed off with the evasion that Spenser and Sidney happened to be ready to write poetry by 1579 and Marlowe and Shakespeare to write dramatic poetry a few years later. Nor should I expect my troublesome querist to be satisfied by the answer that prosodically and rhetorically the language needed a good deal of discipline after the fifteenth century before it could become a fit instrument for epic and tragedy; that when we look at the verse—other than lyric verse—written in England about the year 1500, we ought not to be surprised if eighty years of trial and error, of violent experiment in the use of tropes and figures, of feverish importation of foreign words and phrases, proverbs and images and metres, were necessary before verse could be put upon its feet again. I should expect the man who put so unanswerable a question to pay more heed to the view that the revival of poetry was delayed by the political and theological troubles of the mid-century, troubles which were indeed serious in a society monarchical and aristocratic, when poets depended upon the patronage of the great (unless they were themselves the great) and even the common players— if they were anything more than strolling players— looked to the Court for profits and prestige. By the fifteen-eighties the Elizabethan settlement of State and Church was assured, the country was prospering, and in taking stock the nation was entitled to look to the past with pride and to the future with confidence.

But the poet may be there and ready for dramatic poetry, yet find no players capable of interpreting his lines, no theatre in which they may be worthily spoken, no audience—other than an academic or reading audience—to attend to his lines. That this was so about the year 1580 we have the testimony of Edmund Howes writing some thirty-five years later when most of the plays upon which we set a value today had already been acted. In his continuation of Stow's *Annals*, under the year 1583, Howes observes:

Comedians and stage-players of former time were very poor and ignorant in respect of these of this time: but being now grown very skilful and exquisite actors for all matters, they were entertained into the service of divers great lords: out of which companies there were twelve of the best chosen, and, at the request of Sir Francis Walsingham, they were sworn the Queen's servants and were allowed wages and liveries as grooms of the chamber: and until this year 1583, the Queen had no players. Among these twelve players were two rare men, viz. Thomas [*sic for* Robert] Wilson, for a quick, delicate, refined, extemporal wit, and Richard Tarlton, for a wondrous plentiful pleasant extemporal wit; he was the wonder of his time. [*margin*] Tarlton so beloved that men use his picture for their signs.

As additional evidence that the status of the common players was rising, the modern historian of the theatre will point to the building between 1576 and 1580 of the first three English theatres, two in Middlesex and one in Surrey, and all three beyond reach of the jurisdiction of the City of London; three theatres, not counting the inn-yards, for a population not exceeding a quarter of a million. In these and other events of the time we may see signs that under the protection of the Privy Council the common players were winning, slowly and not without setbacks, the long-drawn-out struggle against the civic authorities and the stricter sort of London ministers. Wilson and Tarlton and their fellows in the 'quality' were no vagrants or strolling actors, but servants of the Queen; and from 1583 till the closing of the theatres London was never without at least one company of professional actors with a stake in the country and decent standards of craftsmanship. Touring the country towns in the summer, rehearsing and performing their new plays in the autumn in the London suburbs, in the winter moving nearer to the heart of London (when the City could not keep them out), and with that shining goal before them—the glory and the profit of acting before the Court itself, they were more in touch with the nation at all levels of taste and intelligence, and in all classes of society, in City, Court, and Country, than any English actors at any other time.

Here, then, by 1580 are the theatres and the actors. But although the Queen's reign is half over, where still are the dramatists? There is, as Howes reminds us, Robert Wilson, dramatist as well as actor; but however much Howes may praise his 'quick, delicate, refined, extemporal wit', we shall not find in Wilson's two plays of the fifteen-eighties the poetry we are looking for. The subject-matter of his earlier and better play, *The Three Ladies of London*, is sufficiently indicated by the stage-direction

'Enter Simony and Usury hand in hand'—they are in league with Fraud and Davy Dissimulation—and Wilson's satire directed through these allegorical types at the poor abuses of the time is at once shrewd and outspoken. But the verse falters and staggers when it does not jog-trot, for Wilson is too fond of twelves and fourteeners, metres with little past and with little future; and the language is only vivid when he is drawing upon the colloquial and proverbial phrases of his day.

When, then, did poetry come to the drama? Candour compels me to admit that Oxford led the way, for of those young university men who turned professional dramatists in the fifteen-eighties with such important consequences to our drama, Peele of Christ Church, and Lyly of Magdalen were first off the mark. If *The Arraignment of Paris* is not our first dramatic piece which is indisputably the work of a poet, I do not know what is, and it was written at any time between 1579 and the year of publication, 1584. Peele is the one university wit whom we know to have taken an active part in academic drama. Whether Marlowe of Corpus Christi or Greene of St. John's and Clare Hall employed themselves at Cambridge in the writing, acting, or producing of academic drama we do not know, but Oxford thought well enough of Peele to bring him back in 1583, four years after he had gone down, to produce two Latin plays by his friend William Gager for the entertainment at Christ Church of Prince Alasco of Poland.

But if Oxford's George Peele led the way, he would hardly have done so if a Cambridge poet had not shown the way. Spenser has left us no plays, yet we cannot doubt that *The Shepheardes Calender* of 1579 and later *The Faerie Queene*, undramatic as they are, affected dramatic verse and rhetoric in a manner as profound as it was beneficial. Nor do we come near to estimating what young dramatists like Peele and Marlowe owed to Spenser if we confine ourselves to obvious borrowings. That there *are* obvious borrowings—of names of characters, of diction and phrasing, indeed in *Tamburlaine* of whole passages—is helpful, but the real debt is more vital. A later Cambridge poet observed that he never sat down to compose poetry without reading Spenser for a considerable time previously. Perhaps we should not have suspected this of Thomas Gray if he had not told us. George Peele has not told us that he tuned his ear to Spenser, but we know it without his telling us; and for an English poet in the early fifteen-eighties about to write his first piece, and striving to breathe grace and life into the stiffness of English dramatic verse, there was no better discipline than to sit down and read *The Shepheardes Calender*. No doubt it is inferior Spenser, but no doubt parts of it are immeasurably better than any other contemporary poetry then in print. There was very much that would not carry over into drama, but there was much that would; and these Elizabethans did not think of themselves as either non-dramatic poets or dramatic poets, but as poets. Their strong sense of decorum guided them in the choice of style and metre for the kind of poem or dramatic poem they were writing. And Peele for *his* diploma piece, *The Arraignment of Paris*, could learn much from Spenser's diploma piece: a virtuosity in metrical experiment and in variety of tone, a decorum of style, a melody more than ordinary, a melody only possible to a man bred to Latin and the rhetoric of the schools but conscious of the necessity of transcending rhetoric by giving pride of place to the nature and custom of his own language. Spenser's schoolmaster, Richard Mulcaster, said in 1582: 'I honour the Latin, but I worship the English'; and again he wrote in words which may suggest to us yet another reason why poetry came to drama, and to English non-lyrical verse, about this time: 'this period in our time seemeth to be the perfitest period in our English tongue . . . there is in our tongue great and sufficient stuff for Art.'

It must be acknowledged that Peele did not fulfil the promise of his earliest play. Did he, like Spenser and yet greater poets, begin with pastoral while dreaming of more ambitious flights to come? Alas, he was incapable of tragedy, and he left behind him only two more things that surprise us by their merit. The one is a lyric exquisitely adapted in tone and temper to the occasion for which it was written, the retirement of Sir Henry Lee as the official champion of the Queen, the lyric which opens with the famous lines:

His golden locks time hath to silver turn'd;
  O time too swift, O swiftness never ceasing!
His youth 'gainst time and age hath ever spurn'd,
  But spurn'd in vain; youth waneth by increasing:
Beauty, strength, youth, are flowers but fading seen;
Duty, faith, love, are roots, and ever green.

And the other work of his which surprises us by its merit is that 'pleasant conceited Comedy', *The Old Wives Tale*, with its 'manifold variety of invention', a play in which poetry and prose, romance and satire, folk-lore, fantasy and realism, sense and non-sense, exist together and enrich each other, a play in which there is not a speech which may not fall sweetly and naturally from an actor's lips. As late as 1589 Thomas Nashe told both universities that Peele was—after Spenser—'the chief supporter of pleasance now living, the *Atlas* of Poetry, and *primus verborum Artifex*'. We can see what Nashe meant, and to a young poet in the fifteen-eighties Peele's verbal and rhythmical felicities were something to be thankful for.

> Hark Flora, Faunus, here is melody,
> A charm of birds and more than ordinary.

But test Peele on a sage and serious subject, and how lamentably does he fail. Ancient Pistol's slightly inaccurate quotation from *The Battle of Alcazar*—'Feed and be fat, my fair Calipolis'—is no unfair comment on the crudities of that play; it has all the rant of *Tamburlaine* without the genius. His rambling chronicle play *Edward I*, as I should like to think, exhibits in some of its serious scenes a bathos of situation, a decrepitude of language, to which no university wit was capable of sinking. It has come down to us in a bad text for some of which Peele cannot be held responsible. As for *David and Bethsabe*, also a chronicle play and also surviving in a corrupt text, it is decorum that it should be uniformly serious, but it is not decorum that it should be uniformly dull. Its occasional beauties are incidental. If we accept Pope's distinction between verses that are soft and verses that are sweet, verses that may be very effeminate and verses that are far from being so, then Peele's verses in *David and Bethsabe* are soft, not sweet. And when a strong situation demands that he raise the tone of his verse, he fails to achieve that other quality which Pope so much admired—a Roman *rotunditas versuum*.

When Peele wrote tragedy or history, he was 'o'erparted'. The environment which would have given him the best vent for his dramatic talent was that in which Lyly flourished. *The Arraignment of Paris* is a court play: it combines the theme of the Judgement of Paris with the pastoral theme of Paris and Oenone, and it ends with a masque-like tribute to the Queen. The few fragments that have survived of his pastoral play, *The Hunting of Cupid*, suggest that it was in his best vein. *The Old Wives Tale* has also some of the marks of a court play. It is full of spectacle and song, and it stands alone in its age as a play acted by adult actors, yet designed, so it would seem, not for the bare boards of the public stage, but for a stage with simultaneous settings, houses of painted canvas each representing a fixed locality, the scene shifting from house to house as the action demanded, the same multiple setting for which Lyly designed his comedies. Peele's gifts lay in the quieter graces of poetry and comedy; his was not the robust genius which could fill the public theatre with poetry and passion. What the stage was still in need of was a dramatist who could write a play on a serious theme in verses that combined sweetness (in Pope's favourable sense of that word) and *rotunditas*. That dramatist appeared in 1587, and if his *rotunditas* was Elizabethan rather than Roman, it was the more acceptable to his audience.

The eldest son of a shoemaker of Canterbury, Marlowe had no advantages of birth in an age when gentility was so sought after that the distinctions between 'yeoman', 'gentleman', and 'esquire' were already confused. With the change of two words in Baldock's speech in *Edward II* we may make Marlowe say:

> My name is *Marlowe*, and my gentry
> I fetcht from *Cambridge*, not from Heraldry.

While some purists were inclined to doubt it, William Segar of the College of Heralds, it is satisfactory to note, admitted that a scholar having continued the study of good learning and aspired to a degree in schools was not to be denied the rank of gentleman. Born in 1564, two months before Shakespeare, Marlowe left the King's School, Canterbury, for Corpus Christi College in 1580, held his scholarship for the maximum period of six years, and in March 1587 was permitted to supplicate for the degree of Master of Arts. Time has little regard for posterity in choosing what it will devour and what it will preserve. It has preserved the sums which Marlowe spent on food and drink during his residence at Corpus: it has devoured all memory of his Cambridge friendships. What did he think of Spenser's friend, Gabriel Harvey, then of Trinity Hall, or did he not think of him at all? And, what we should like to know more, when did he meet his slightly younger contemporary, Thomas Nashe of St. John's, the man whose name was to appear with his on the title-page of *Dido Queen of Carthage*, the man who never abused him in his life and after his death wrote affectionately of 'poor deceased Kit Marlowe' and praised the poet and his work in elegiac verses which have been lost, alas, since the mid-eighteenth century?

How normal, how uneventful does Marlowe's life at Cambridge appear if we judge it solely by the academic records! All that may be urged against him—and this very doubtfully—is that a scholar on Archbishop Parker's foundation might have been expected to take orders. But history has preserved two pieces of information which shatter this normality to fragments. The one is the remarkable minute in the registers of the Privy Council for 29 June 1587, denying the report that 'Christopher Morley was determined to have gone beyond the seas to

Reims and there to remain', testifying that he had behaved himself discreetly and had done the Queen good service, and requesting that he be furthered in the degree he was to take the next Commencement: 'Because it was not her Majesty's pleasure that any one employed as he had been in matters touching the benefit of his Country should be defamed by those that are ignorant in th' affairs he went about.' Whatever the feeling of his college and his university, the intervention was effective and Marlowe was given in July the degree of Master of Arts for which the 'supplicat' had been signed in March. On what government service he had been employed we do not know, but it was of such a nature as to bring him under suspicion of leanings towards Roman Catholicism. It is the first hint we have that he had become involved in the underworld of Elizabethan politics; as the last hint is the scene in that house at Deptford on 30 May 1593 where the poet met a violent death in the presence of the secret agent Robert Poley and two of Poley's associates, three men of whom so much has been discovered in recent years and nothing good.

What also makes Marlowe one of the most extraordinary young men that ever went down from a university is that before he took his Master's degree he had already written the first part of *Tamburlaine*, if not the second, had transformed the nature of English dramatic verse, and had provided the public stage with the passion and poetry it was in need of.

By 1587, then, the shoemaker's son of Canterbury had done much to recommend himself to the attention of his betters. He had taken his Master's degree, thereby establishing some sort of claim to gentility; more important for worldly advancement was the fact that while he had rejected one means of advancement, the Church, he had won the favourable notice of the Privy Council. Moreover, two plays of his had been acted with applause upon the London stage; and in an age when eloquence was revered by all and poetry by many, this counted for much. By poetry and poetry alone the bailiff's son of Stratford was soon to earn the patronage of the Earl of Southampton.

A very few years before Marlowe took his degree, another Cambridge man of humble birth, another *novus homo* or 'gentleman of the first head', was jotting down for his own guidance the rules by which a man might become the architect of his own fortunes. The prince's court, Gabriel Harvey observed, was the only mart of preferment and honour: 'Give me entrance, and let me alone. Give me footing, and I will find elbow room.' With 'a hot invincible mind and a hot durable body', with 'bold courtly speaking and bold industrious doing', he promised himself a glorious career.

He that would be thought a Man, or seem anything worth, must be a great Doer and a great Speaker. He is a Cipher, and but a peakgoose, that is neither of both: he is the right man, that is both: he that cannot be both, let him be one at least, if he mean to be accounted anybody. Or farewell all hope of value.

In these private notes meant only for his own eyes, the ropemaker's son of Saffron Walden was setting himself down, as Professor Moore Smith observed, as 'the Renaissance man pure and simple, and in him we see the full influence of the Renaissance more clearly than in any other Englishman known to us'.

In 1576, before Harvey's hopes of advancement had been dashed by the follies of his nature, and especially perhaps by his want of common sense, he noted in the margin of one of his books that Tamburlaine from 'a lusty stout herdsman' rose to become 'a most valiant and invincible prince'. It is easy to see why Tamburlaine seemed to Harvey a good exemplar. Can we guess at the reason why Tamburlaine seemed to Marlowe a suitable theme for his first play? That Marlowe thought of Tamburlaine as 'a most valiant and invincible prince' is, I think, certain. The Tamburlaine who first captured Marlowe's imagination is the Tamburlaine of the first part; for the second part, in which Tamburlaine is defeated by his enemy death, is an afterthought. Those who think otherwise are forced to consider *Tamburlaine* as a ten-act play, a desperate argument, for only by some very special pleading can the statement in the prologue to the second part be interpreted as meaning anything else than that the success of the first part induced the dramatist to write a sequel,

> Where death cuts off the progress of his pomp,
> And murderous Fates throws all his triumphs down.

Even if Marlowe did conceive *Tamburlaine* as a ten-act play, Part I would still be the unit of dramatic performance, of the two-to-three-hour traffic of the stage. There is no epilogue warning the audience that ambition does not triumph in the end and that they are to return the next day or the next week to see the proof of it; and even if there were such an epilogue, it would be in flat contradiction to the play. The Tamburlaine who first attracted Marlowe was the man of humble birth who rises from victory to victory to the noon or meridian of his fortunes, where the dramatist leaves him a happy warrior and a happy lover.

Possibly we may better guess why this theme

kindled in Marlowe's mind if we examine one of the many accounts of Tamburlaine which he read. Let us choose not the *Silva* of Pedro Mexia, not the *Vita* of Perondinus, not the Turkish chronicle of Lonicerus, not Thomas Fortescue's *Forest, or Collection of Histories*, which editors have taken to be his English source, but another English life of Tamburlaine, closer to Marlowe's play than Fortescue's, and strangely neglected until recent years.

George Whetstone's *English Mirror* was published in 1586, the year in which Whetstone fought with Sidney at Zutphen. It was the very year, we may suppose, when Marlowe's thoughts were beginning to turn to this theme. Whetstone wrote his book when a Spanish invasion was already imminent. 'Seen and allowed' by the official censors, dedicated to the Queen and the nobility, its claim to be 'a work safely and necessary to be read of every good subject' was amply merited, for it is a patriotic call for political and religious unity. There could be nothing more orthodox. Whetstone declared that of all countries England alone was in peace and prosperity, alone 'free from feeling the vengeance of envy, and many enemies'; and he urged his countrymen to be 'thankful for this divine protection' and to take warning from the punishments which God had visited upon England in the past and upon the countries of Europe in the present by reason of the sinful dissensions of Christians. Of all the scourges whom God had sent, the most notable in recent history had been Tamburlaine, and because Whetstone regarded Tamburlaine as the instrument of God's anger, he could give of him—as does his source, Pedro Mexia—what is on the whole a sympathetic account. 'In his army was never found mutine. He was wise, liberal, and rewarded every soldier with his desert. There is no remembrance of a greater army than this.' The battle in which he forced Bajazeth, Emperor of the Turks, to raise the siege of Constantinople was the fiercest battle 'that in any age was foughten'. Bajazeth's fate, to be carried about in an iron cage and fed from the fragments of Tamburlaine's table, is used as evidence not of Tamburlaine's cruelty but of the uncertainty of worldly fortunes: the moral is that of the lines from Seneca's *Thyestes* which Marlowe was to quote in *Edward II* and which Jonson was to use for the final couplet of *Sejanus*:

> For, whom the morning saw so great, and high,
> Thus low and little, 'fore the 'even doth lie.

The only reference to Tamburlaine's cruelty is near the end where Tamburlaine commands the slaughter of women and children sent out from a besieged city to beg for mercy on the third day of warning when 'the gates of compassion were closed'.

And in truth [observes Whetstone], Tamburlaine although he was endued with many excellencies and virtues, yet it seemed by his cruelty that God raised him to chasten the kings and proud people of the earth.

Here in Tamburlaine Marlowe found the greatest example in the modern world of the successful conqueror, the clear-eyed man who knew the goal to which he aspired and the means by which he might attain it. Tamburlaine had, wrote Whetstone, 'a ruling desire'. The phrase has a modern ring, and indeed the earliest example of 'ruling' in the sense of 'predominating' supplied by the *Oxford English Dictionary* is Pope's 'ruling passion' (1732). By 'a ruling desire' Whetstone meant 'a desire for rule', not a consuming passion, but in *his* Tamburlaine as in Marlowe's the desire to rule *is* a ruling passion, a passion for 'The sweet fruition of an earthly crown' and all the power and the glory which that brings with it. All Marlowe's heroes have a ruling passion in Pope's sense of the phrase, even his one heroine Dido, even his one impotent hero Edward II: but Tamburlaine alone achieves his desire, and in Part I, at any rate, he is not cheated of his desire.

If there is one passage above all in Whetstone which might have stirred Marlowe to the choice of

this theme, it is this: 'notwithstanding the poverty
of his parents, even from his infancy he had a reaching and an imaginative mind; the strength and
comeliness of his body answered the haughtiness
of his heart.' Whether Marlowe was strong and
comely in body, we do not know; but how apt is
all the rest to what we know or may surmise of him!
A young man of humble birth, who had already
done some service to the State, who knew that to
make his way in the world in which he lived he
must be both 'a great doer and a great speaker',
could have found no more congenial subject for the
first-fruits of his genius than this greatest example
in the modern world of the successful conqueror,
the man of action whose eloquence is part of his
success as a man of action. The two opening scenes
of his play point the contrast between the man who
is both doer and speaker and the man who is
neither, between the 'peakgoose' Mycetes, who
finds himself aggrieved,

> Yet insufficient to express the same,
> For it requires a great and thundering speech:
> Good brother, tell the cause unto my lords;
> I know you have a better wit than I;

and Tamburlaine who is never at a loss for 'great
and thundering speech' or for persuasive speech,
and who at his first appearance—against the advice

of his lieutenants—prefers speech to action and by his oratory wins a bloodless victory over his new ally Theridamas and exacts the tribute:

> Not Hermes, prolocutor to the gods,
> Could use persuasions more pathetical.

The play is hardly under way, yet Tamburlaine has shown himself to possess all the attributes of a ruler, a majesty in action and a majesty in words, 'working words' and actions that 'top his speech'. Sir Philip Sidney's commendation of his Arcadian gallant was that he 'durst and knew'. The Renaissance man must have courage *and* brains, haughtiness of heart *and* a reaching and imaginative mind. And to Marlowe—or shall we say more guardedly to the Marlowe of 1586–7—Tamburlaine was the supreme type of such a man.

II

TAMBURLAINE

TAMBURLAINE, Part 1, the 'first heir' of Marlowe's dramatic invention with the possible exception of *Dido*, is a work of art deliberately wrought. It is no *opus septem dierum*. The 'raptures . . . all air and fire' which make the lyrical parts of the play so memorable are compatible with much careful attention to structure and dramatic effect. The researches of Miss Seaton and others have shown that he read voraciously, both in books and maps, to prepare himself for this work and built up his play deliberately from a memory of wide-flung sources. The pains that he took are evidence of the fascination which the theme had for him. Just possibly he revised both parts between the date of performance in 1587 and the date of publication in one octavo volume in 1590: for there are borrowings from two works not yet published in 1587. One of these is *The Faerie Queene*. That part of Spenser's poem from which his borrowings are most striking and most certain, the seventh and eighth cantos of the first book, he could have seen in manuscript. In these cantos Arthur makes his first appearance in the poem, and they form an intelligible and vivid extract which would cut a pretty figure in any commonplace-book. In borrowing from a work not his immediate source Marlowe is doing what Shakespeare seldom did, and never on this scale; but in so doing he was no plagiarist. He picked up a feather or two with which to plume the wings of his invention. His other borrowing, a technical passage from Paul Ive's *Practice of Fortification* of 1589, is more satisfactorily explained by revision; and if Marlowe took an interest in their publication, it would explain how the publisher Richard Jones came by so good a text of two popular plays still in the repertory of the Admiral's players. It is the publisher, however, not the dramatist, who signs the address to the reader. We have to wait for another decade—until the generation of Jonson, Chapman, Marston, and Dekker—for examples of popular plays introduced to the reader by the dramatists themselves. Jones's preface is truly remarkable not because he commends the eloquence of the poet and the worthiness of the matter but because he proclaims that he has purposely omitted 'some fond and frivolous gestures' as 'far unmeet for the matter' and 'a great disgrace to so honourable and stately a history'. Is there another example of an Elizabethan publisher who in the interests of good art excised from a popular drama passages which had proved successful upon the stage? That sort of censorship is rare in any age.

Whether Marlowe's blank verse was the earliest to meet with success upon the popular stage we cannot say. Kyd's *Spanish Tragedy* cannot be assigned to a more precise date than the mid or late fifteen-eighties. It may be argued that because Kyd shows no sign of having heard the tune of *Tamburlaine*, therefore he wrote before Marlowe. While the fiery spirit informing the verse of *Tamburlaine* is inimitable, the pace and the resonance of his lines, the imagery and diction, left their mark upon many an imitator: but not upon Kyd. Between *The Spanish Tragedy* and *Tamburlaine* there is nothing in common except the choice of blank verse. The one is a tragedy of revenge—Seneca turned Elizabethan and adapted to Elizabethan ears and the Elizabethan theatre—written by a man who was but a small poet yet had a talent for conceiving strong situations in terms of the theatre, and a gift for rhetoric which reveals the competent craftsman working upon materials available to his age. The other is no tragedy at all but an heroic play, written by a poet who is already the master of rhetoric, not its slave, and in verse which matches in power the energy of the conception, verse which at its greatest has the unpredictability of genius and 'surprises us by its fine excess'.

The Prologue to *Tamburlaine*, Part I, is the proud manifesto of a new poet conscious of bringing to the public stage an unaccustomed dignity of theme and style:

From jigging veins of rhyming mother wits,
And such conceits as clownage keeps in pay,
We'll lead you to the stately tent of war,
Where you shall hear the Scythian Tamburlaine
Threatening the world with high astounding terms. . . .

The reference to 'such conceits as clownage keeps in pay' suggests that whatever may have been the 'fond and frivolous gestures' which the publisher omitted they were not the conceits of clownage. We may conjecture that what has disappeared is not a clown like the Strumbo and Bullithrumble of *Locrine* and *Selimus*, two plays much influenced by *Tamburlaine*, but more speeches of scornful comedy in those scenes in which Tamburlaine taunts Mycetes or Bajazeth, and Zenocrate Zabina, the only scenes to which fragments of prose now adhere. While we may think these scenes 'of an ill mingle with the rest', as Dryden's Lisideius said of similar scenes in *Sejanus* and *Catiline*, yet their scorn and their attachment to the action distinguish them from scenes of mere clownage. For the rest, Marlowe mirrors in his 'tragic glass' the 'stately tent of war', and his style keeps decorum.

Against this style two main objections have been made: that it is bombastic: that it is monotonous. Perhaps his answer to the charge of bombast would have been that 'the high astounding terms' of Tamburlaine are dramatic, that 'A great and thundering speech' is required of a hero who is 'The only fear and terror of the world' and whose faith in his destiny is such that he believes himself to hold the Fates fast bound in iron chains. Marlowe knew what to say. Did he not know how to say it? Above all, did he not know how to say it in terms of his actors and his theatre? When we read plays which we have no opportunity of seeing, or no opportunity of seeing acted with the skilled attention to pronunciation and gesture which alone can give them life upon the stage, we too often forget—however much we may be on our guard—that the dramatist's lines were written to be spoken and heard, to be spoken in a public theatre and to be heard by an audience drawn from all classes of society. Marlowe was young when he wrote *Tamburlaine*: he was still young when he wrote his last play and his last poem: yet while extravagance of language and situation are not absent from his later work, it is nowhere so marked as in *Tamburlaine*. Aristotle observed that hyperbole by reason of its vehemence was a figure more appropriate to the young than to the old, but the style of *Tamburlaine* is vehement and hyperbolical not so much because Marlowe was young as because he was keeping decorum. He was writing in passion of a man of passion, and his figures are those of passion. When the hyperboles are those of Tamburlaine's enemies, they are weighted with the irony of impending catastrophe: when they are Tamburlaine's, they are informed by his zest for life and insatiable ambition. The setting and the imagery as much as the language and the rhythm are proportionate to the theme. And if declamation sometimes roars, passion does not sleep.

Too little justice has been done to Marlowe's sense of decorum or to the variety of his work. Charles Lamb observed, in a conversation reported by Crabb Robinson, that Marlowe's works are all of a different kind, and it is a true observation. We are apt to forget this because we think too much of his heroes, of the *amour de l'impossible*, and so on. While every play of his exhibits at least one character with a ruling passion, in every play the style is adapted to the tone and temper of the changing theme. He was not a dramatist who was content to go on repeating the same effects. The style and method of progression in his next play, *The Jew of Malta*, are entirely different from what we find in

Tamburlaine. And who can say what a poet might have done next who spent his last months (as the evidence suggests that he did) in writing works so different from each other and from his earlier works as *Doctor Faustus* and *Hero and Leander?* Never again after *Tamburlaine* did Marlowe have occasion to make his audiences travel by card and map through the known world, to splash his lines with geographical colour and sonority and spaciousness. His addiction to classical mythology in *Tamburlaine* is not so obviously appropriate to his theme, and is perhaps a sign that he was writing with all his learning, and especially all his Ovid, in his head: it does not disappear from his later plays, but there it is much less prominent. And his imagery is never again so meteoric, meteoric in the wide sense as having reference to any atmospheric phenomena, whether comets, exhalations, meteors (in the narrower sense), lightnings, thunderbolts, all fit accompaniments to this Scourge and Wrath of God.

Marlowe's play retained its popularity for a generation, but in that forcing-bed the Elizabethan theatre its style soon became outmoded. Marlowe himself in his later plays did much to make it outmoded. His 'Holla ye pampered jades of Asia!' shares with old Hieronimo's 'What outcries pluck me from my naked bed?' the unenviable distinction of being the most parodied line in Elizabethan drama. 'Huff-cap terms' and 'thundering threats' —Tamburlaine's no less than Hotspur's

> By heaven, methinks it were an easy leap
> To pluck bright honour from the pale-faced moon—

these are easy game for the satirist, and most of the references to *Tamburlaine* in the years that followed Marlowe's death are to the furious gestures and the stalking steps of actors who played the part with a tempest in their tongues and thunder in their heels. What an irony of fate it is that this poet's plays, *The Jew of Malta* and *Doctor Faustus* even more than *Tamburlaine*, plays so original and daring in conception, often so sublime in expression, should have descended to the dregs of the acting profession and become fare for the rowdy Shrovetide audiences of the London populace! The actors betrayed him with too much force.

The other charge that has been levelled against the style of *Tamburlaine* is that it is monotonous, if indeed this is not the same charge: for there is nothing more monotonous than sustained and noisy bombast. Oddly enough, the charge of monotony is made in its extreme form by one of Marlowe's greatest admirers, by the critic who claimed that

Marlowe differed from such dramatists as Peele and Greene 'not in degree, but in kind; not as an eagle differs from wrens or titmice, but as an eagle differs from frogs or tadpoles', by the critic who saluted Marlowe as 'the greatest discoverer, the most daring and inspired pioneer, in all our poetic literature'. It was this critic who wrote that *Tamburlaine* is monotonous 'in the general roll and flow of its stately and sonorous verse through a noisy wilderness of perpetual bluster and slaughter', and that the majestic and exquisite excellence of various lines and passages may relieve, but cannot be allowed to redeem, 'the stormy monotony of Titanic truculence which blusters like a simoom through the noisy course of its ten fierce acts'. I need not say that this critic is Swinburne. That the reader of *Tamburlaine*—and how many of us can boast that we are more than readers?—is conscious of this monotone may not be denied, yet Marlowe has done much, and done it deliberately, to avoid monotony. To think of him as a non-dramatic poet forced by the circumstances of his age into writing dramatic poetry alien to the true nature of his genius is seriously to underestimate his dramatic gifts. There is much to be admired in the manner in which he exhibits in five acts the rise of the Scythian shepherd to be the greatest ruler in the world. From the capture of Zenocrate and the stratagems by which Tamburlaine makes himself King of Persia in Acts I and II to the hero's rise to the zenith of his fortunes in Act V with the capture of Damascus, the death of Bajazeth, the defeat and capture of the Soldan, and the crowning of Zenocrate, the interest works up to a climax. This interest Marlowe has attempted to vary when possible, and when he makes the attempt he is almost always independent of his sources. One attempt we have already noted: the contrast in the opening scenes between Tamburlaine and the weak-witted and inarticulate Mycetes. Another is the scene, elegiac in tone, in which Tamburlaine over-hears the attempt of Agydas to alienate Zenocrate (III. ii). It is a scene which slows down for a time the speed of the play. It is a scene of some suspense, and in a play where Tamburlaine's victories follow inevitably one upon another suspense comes seldom. And it is the one scene in either part in which Tamburlaine enters and does not speak: it is as if Marlowe were bent on showing that Tamburlaine was as powerful in silence as in speech. Above all, there is the variety given by the invention of Zeno-crate. It is Zenocrate, the symbol of beauty and compassion, who turns Tamburlaine into a lover when he might have been merely a conqueror; it is

Zenocrate who sets up a conflict between Honour
and Love in a mind otherwise undivided and single;
it is Zenocrate who speaks or who inspires some
of the lyrical passages which contrast so markedly
with the ruthless clangour of much of the heroic
verse; it is Zenocrate who exacts from this all-
conquering conqueror an admission of defeat.

> What is beauty, saith my sufferings, then?
> If all the pens that ever poets held
> Had fed the feeling of their masters' thoughts,
> And every sweetness that inspir'd their hearts,
> Their minds and muses on admired themes;
> If all the heavenly quintessence they still
> From their immortal flowers of poesy,
> Wherein as in a mirror we perceive
> The highest reaches of a human wit—
> If these had made one poem's period,
> And all combin'd in beauty's worthiness,
> Yet should there hover in their restless heads
> One thought, one grace, one wonder, at the least,
> Which into words no virtue can digest.

In this and other passages of lyrical incantation
Marlowe was writing such poetry as had never
been heard on the English stage before and has
seldom been heard since. To those who say that
this poetry is undramatic I would answer that no
poetry is undramatic that brings all sorts and conditions of men to the theatre and forces them to listen.

So far I have been speaking chiefly of the first part of *Tamburlaine*, though much that I have said may be applied to the second part and to Marlowe in general. Of the second part I shall say little. All critics agree that this sequel is a falling off, though some recent critics have found here too evidence of Marlowe's dramatic gifts. Most of the material from his sources he had used up in his first play, and he had little left for a second part except the death of Tamburlaine. 'In the end', writes Whetstone tersely in his *English Mirror*, 'this great personage, without disgrace of fortune, after sundry great victories, by the course of nature died.' To sustain a five-act play much had to be invented or borrowed from other sources: the treachery of the Christian Sigismund King of Hungary to the Turk Orcanes; the love of Theridamas for the captured Olympia (III. iv and IV. ii), an episode which corresponds in its elegiac tone and in its placing in the play to the Agydas episode in Part I (III. ii), and seems deliberately placed to give a contrast in speed and in tone. Even the notorious business of the chariot drawn by the captive kings, the 'pampered jades of Asia', is not found in the chronicles of Tamburlaine: was it suggested by the reports of Sesostris, the great king of Egypt, who yoked kings and princes together in chains and forced them to

draw his wagon? Add that Marlowe invented the
escape of Bajazeth's son and the character of Tamburlaine's cowardly and despicable son. Above all,
add Zenocrate and Tamburlaine's furious madness
after her death.

In Part I the interest is wholly in Tamburlaine:
in Part II much of the interest is sluiced off into
other channels. The difference may be illustrated
by a minute point of dramatic technique. In each
scene of Part I the characters are already possessed
with news of what has happened in the previous
scene: there is no recapitulation, no showing the
immediate impact of Tamburlaine's victories upon
his victims. For Marlowe's interest is not in the
victims but in Tamburlaine. Only the opening scene
recounts past actions: the rest is present and to
come. Contrast Part II and especially that scene in
which a messenger brings news to the Turks of
the Christians' breach of faith: it is a dramatic
scene and the speech of scornful anger which Marlowe puts into the mouth of Orcanes when the news
is brought to him is one of the most deeply religious
utterances in the whole range of Elizabethan drama.
Orcanes, a noble character, is no foil to Tamburlaine as was Mycetes, but a rival; this is one of
many signs that Tamburlaine's fortunes, which rose
to their zenith in Part I, are now falling. Other

signs are the escape of Bajazeth's son, Callapine, the cowardice of Tamburlaine's son and, above all, the death of Zenocrate.

With all their imperfections what a remarkable achievement are these two plays for a young man of twenty-three! In conception and in style they are daringly original. Are they as original and as daring in the view of life which they present? It is here that the question of Marlowe's character and beliefs raises its head. I rather wish that I might say nothing of them, but some critics have attached so much importance to his private beliefs for the interpretation of his plays—as I think, too much importance—that I must say something.

We may begin with that day in the summer of 1589 when William Bradley, son of the keeper of the Bishop Inn just opposite Staple Inn, asked for sureties of the peace against the poet and dramatist Thomas Watson, against Watson's brother-in-law Hugh Swift, and against John Allen probably the brother of the actor Edward. Not long before, Hugh Swift had sought sureties of the peace against George Orrell, son of a victualler, who was later to take a prominent part in the Essex rebellion and to be described in a letter to Robert Cecil as 'a most desperate rakehell'. The sequel is surprising and fatal. On 18 September Marlowe and William

Bradley were fighting together in Hog Lane, near
Finsbury Fields, a noted duelling-place. Watson
who happened to be at hand—we have only Watson's and Marlowe's evidence: in the nature of the
case we cannot have Bradley's—Watson drew his
sword in order to separate the combatants, where-
upon Bradley called out to him: 'Art thou now
come? Then I will have a bout with thee.' Watson
struck Bradley a mortal blow, he and Marlowe
were arrested on a charge of murder, the jury
brought in a verdict of self-defence, and Marlowe
was released after a few days in Newgate, Watson
after a few months. On the bench was Sir Roger
Manwood whose epitaph Marlowe was to write,
as he was three years later to write a Latin dedica-
tion recommending the posthumously published
verses of his friend Watson to the Countess of
Pembroke, the patroness-general in her age, 'Poet-
arum nostri temporis . . . Musa.' Both Watson and
Marlowe were then living in the Liberty of Norton
Folgate not far from the Theatre in Shoreditch.
Marlowe was still living in the same neighbour-
hood, and was still being described as 'generosus',
when in May 1592 he was bound over to keep the
peace against the constable and the under-constable
of Holywell Street, Shoreditch. These are the discoveries of Professor Eccles. If we add to these

incidents what the researches of Dr. Hotson have revealed of the last scene of all in Marlowe's strange eventful history, the manner of his death at Deptford on 30 May 1593, we may be tempted to exclaim, as was Matthew Arnold after reading the private life of the author of *The Necessity of Atheism*, 'What a set! What a world!'

To these must be added the many accusations of atheism brought against Marlowe by those who knew him, or professed to know him. Two of these he read in print in the pamphlets of the jealous, petulant, and malicious Robert Greene. In 1588 Greene attributed the failure of one of his plays to the fact that 'I could not make my verses jet upon the stage in tragical buskins, every word filling the mouth like a fa-burden of Bow-bell, daring God out of heaven with that atheist Tamburlaine'; and, punning on Marlowe's name, he went on to allude to 'such mad scoffing poets, that have poetical spirits as bred of Merlin's race, if there be any in England, that set the end of scholarism in an English blank verse'. These are very bitter words, but not so bitter as those which appeared in Greene's death-bed admonition to Marlowe in his *Groatsworth of Wit* of August 1592, that 'scald trivial lying pamphlet' as Nashe, another of Greene's victims, so justly called it:

Wonder not . . . thou famous gracer of Tragedians, that Greene, who hath said with thee (like the fool in his heart) 'There is no God', should now give glory unto His greatness. . . . Why should thy excellent wit, His gift, be so blinded that thou shouldst give no glory to the giver? Is it pestilent Machiavellian policy that thou hast studied? O peevish folly!

When shortly afterwards the printer–dramatist Henry Chettle found it necessary to publish an apology for the part he had taken in the publication of Greene's pamphlet, he declared that he was not acquainted with the two men who had taken offence —Shakespeare and Marlowe—'and with one of them I care not if I never be'. While he reverenced Marlowe's learning, he observed that he had omitted something of what Greene had written 'in his displeasure' against Marlowe, which 'had it been true, yet to publish it was intolerable'. To the charge of atheism did Greene add the charge of homosexuality?

Greene's evidence, if it stood alone, might be discounted on the grounds of jealousy and malice, but the other evidence, which belongs to the time immediately before and after Marlowe's death, is not so easily disposed of. On 11 May 1593 the Privy Council, disturbed by the setting up in London of 'divers lewd and malicious libels', ordered search to be made for the author. Thomas Kyd was one of those suspected and searched, and among his papers were found abstracts from a book on the Arian heresy. Arrested the next day, he pleaded that the abstracts belonged to Marlowe and were shuffled among his papers, unknown to him, when he and Marlowe were writing together 'in one chamber two years since'. A warrant for Marlowe's arrest at the house of his patron Thomas Walsingham at Scadbury in Kent or wherever he might be found was issued on 18 May, and two days later Marlowe appeared before the Council and was ordered to give daily attendance until licensed to the contrary. We may not assume that Marlowe would not have been able to clear himself of the serious charges which had been brought against him. In those days a friend at court was worth more than a penny in the purse. For all we know he may have cleared himself before he was killed at Deptford ten days later.

The charges against Marlowe and the reports of his conversation are to be found in a statement made by one Richard Baines shortly before Marlowe's death and in two letters from Kyd to Sir John Puckering written after Marlowe's death. It is from Kyd's testimony that we learn that Marlowe in his table talk would jest at the scriptures, gibe at prayers, utter blasphemies against the character of Christ, that he was intemperate and of a cruel heart, and rash in attempting sudden privy injuries to men. Baines gives more detail. A characteristic item in his report of Marlowe's scoffing, taunting speech is: 'That all they that love not tobacco and boys were fools.' Baines alleged that into every company Marlowe came he persuaded men to atheism, and that one Richard Cholmley had confessed that he was one of Marlowe's converts. A document containing charges of atheism against Cholmley is of interest because it associates Marlowe with Raleigh: Marlowe is reported to have told Cholmley that 'he hath read the Atheist lecture to Sir Walter Raleigh and others'. This may be linked with Baines's report that Marlowe had given 'a number of contrarieties out of the Scripture' to some 'great men'. In passing we may note that while Raleigh was a man curious in matters both of divinity and natural philosophy, he made a sharp distinction between reason and revelation, and twenty years later wrote his *History of the World* in the full tide of religious orthodoxy. In short, like Montaigne at a certain stage in his life, he was both sceptic and fideist.

In mitigation of Marlowe's flouting and scoffing conversation it has been urged that what we know of Richard Baines (if he be Richard Baines of the Middle Temple) does not prejudice us in his favour, and that Kyd was writing after the death of a man whom in life he professed to hate, was shaken by disgrace and torture, and anxious at any cost to be restored to the favour of his patron. And yet, as almost any Elizabethan except Marlowe might have said, there is no smoke without fire. There are too many correspondences between these documents for us to suppose that they are mere libels upon the dead. One detail has been corroborated only in recent years. One of the few reported sayings of Marlowe that concern the State and not religion is that he had as good a right to coin as the Queen of England and that he was acquainted with a coiner named Poole, a prisoner in Newgate. We know now that a coiner, John Poole, was in Newgate in 1589 when Marlowe spent some days there.

Interpret everything for the worst and here was a man of a cruel and intemperate heart; malign; wishing and contriving ill for friend and foe alike; a blasphemous heretic and a dangerous rebel. Interpret everything for the best and here was a man beloved and revered by some, and especially by poets, feared and distrusted by others; of great intellectual pride and power yet keenly susceptible to beauty whether of mind or sense; more devoted to ideas than to people, and insatiably curious; not suffering fools gladly, indeed exasperated beyond bearing by dullness and hypocrisy; a shoemaker's son with no tincture in his nature of the gentle craft; finding in human nature in general as much of the knave as the fool; no atheist, but a deist before we had borrowed the word from the French; at once repelled by dogma and fascinated by it, and better read in divinity than any other Elizabethan dramatist. Whatever view is taken, here is a character at the opposite pole to that of his great contemporary, of whom Walter Raleigh has written:

he was 'honest, and of an open and free nature'; and always he is 'the gentle Shakespeare'. If we could make his living acquaintance, we should expect to find in him one of those well-balanced and plastic tempers which enable men to attract something less than their due share of observation and remark as they pass to and fro among their fellows. . . . Every one was more himself for being in the company of Shakespeare. This is not speculation, but truth: without such a gift he could not have come by his knowledge of mankind. Those lofty and severe tempers who, often to their own shame, make others feel abashed and shy, could by no possibility, even if they were dramatically minded, collect the materials of Shakespeare's drama.

Knowing so much, and yet so little, of Marlowe's

character and beliefs, to what use may we put this knowledge in interpreting his plays? Critics who take the view that he was a highly subjective dramatist have been tempted to find in his work many a covert gibe at the orthodoxies of his age. Covert they would have to be, for censorship established a substantial orthodoxy in matters of State and Church. A test case is the noble speech of the Turk Orcanes after news has been brought to him that the Christians have broken faith (2 *Tamburlaine*, ii. ii). The 'papers' to which he refers are the 'articles of peace' which he holds in his hand and tears to pieces as he speaks.

> Can there be such deceit in Christians,
> Or treason in the fleshly heart of man,
> Whose shape is figure of the highest God?
> Then, if there be a Christ, as Christians say,
> But in their deeds deny him for their Christ,
> If he be son to everliving Jove,
> And hath the power of his outstretchèd arm,
> If he be jealous of his name and honour
> As is our holy prophet Mahomet,
> Take here these papers as our sacrifice
> And witness of thy servant's perjury!
> Open, thou shining veil of Cynthia,
> And make a passage from the imperial heaven,
> That he that sits on high and never sleeps,
> Nor in one place is circumscriptible,
> But everywhere fills every continent

With strange infusion of his sacred vigour,
May, in his endless power and purity,
Behold and venge this traitor's perjury!
Thou, Christ, that art esteem'd omnipotent,
If thou wilt prove thyself a perfect God,
Worthy the worship of all faithful hearts,
Be now reveng'd upon this traitor's soul, . . .
To arms, my lords! on Christ still let us cry:
If there be Christ, we shall have victory.

There is nothing unorthodox in the reference to God as in no place circumscriptible and filling every continent 'With strange infusion of his sacred vigour': Professor Kocher, the ablest advocate of the subjectivity of Marlowe's plays, has shown that. But must we feel behind such a phrase as 'if there be a Christ' the sardonic humour of a man delighting to do sudden privy injuries to the Christian religion? It is not necessary, for every word in Orcanes's speech is dramatic, just as dramatic and just as orthodox as the Christian traitor Sigismund's admission of sin and interpretation of defeat as a punishment for sin: 'O just and dreadful punisher of sin.' The wrath of Orcanes is a righteous wrath, and would be accepted as such by Marlowe's audience: for the reproach that many a heathen followed better the precepts of Christ than those who were blessed with the benefits of revealed religion, had been thundered at them from many a pulpit.

The danger of reading private allusions into Marlowe's plays is that we do injury to his dramatic gifts. We are tempted to see him in a false perspective as a frustrated lyric poet instead of the very considerable dramatic poet that he was. We are tempted to forget that a dramatic poet—even an Elizabethan dramatic poet, believing that it is the function of poetry to teach delightfully—may yet be the disinterested artist losing his identity in the stuff which he is turning into art and that a great poet is expressing deeper impulses of his nature than could ever find expression in scoffing conversation with a Richard Baines or a Thomas Kyd. We are also tempted to make his plays out to be more unorthodox than in fact they are. For example, the doctrine that faith may be broken at will with heretics, argued by the Christian Baldwin and in Marlowe's source by a Cardinal, appears again in *The Jew of Malta*, where the Jew with sardonic humour argues that on that principle it can be no sin to deceive a Christian, for 'all are heretics that are not Jews'. Here, say some critics, is another characteristic fling of Marlowe's at the Christian religion. It is true that he does not apply this doctrine in peculiar to the Papists, as did

Dr. John Bridges in a sermon preached at Paul's Cross in 1571, as Shakespeare was to do in *King John* in the words of the Cardinal Pandulph:

> And blessed shall he be that doth revolt
> From his allegiance to an heretic.

The nature of his plots in *Tamburlaine* and *The Jew of Malta* would anyhow compel him to refer to Christians, not to Papists and Protestants. Even so, the passages in these two plays are not so much indictments of Christianity as of human nature, 'treason in the fleshly heart of man'. And if we must accuse Marlowe of blasphemous heresy because he makes his Christians appear at a disadvantage as against his Turk and his Jew, what are we to say of Robert Wilson in his *Three Ladies of London* written about the year 1581? There a Christian merchant doing business in Turkey is so vicious that he proposes to forswear his faith and turn Turk in order to escape the payment of a debt which he owes to a Jewish usurer. There the Jew is so virtuous that he forgives the debt in order that the merchant may not forsake his faith, even though a Christian faith, in so wicked a fashion. And the judge's comment is: 'Jews seek to excel in Christianity and Christians in Jewishness.' If this is heretical, it is as heretical as anything in Marlowe; but of course it is not heretical. Robert Wilson's play claims to be 'a perfect pattern for all estates to look into', and the episode of the Jew and the merchant is an *exemplum*, the kind of *exemplum* which might have been used by any preacher, to expose social corruption and to awaken a slumbering conscience.

With these considerations in mind, let us return to the question: Are these two plays as original and daring in the view of life which they present as they are in conception and in style? It is not impossible to reconcile *The Jew of Malta*, *The Massacre at Paris*, *Edward II*, and of course *Doctor Faustus* with orthodox Elizabethan morality. Each play presents a character of exceptional power seeking exceptional power—Barabas, Guise, Mortimer, Faustus; they are deterred by no scruples from seeking their end, and in seeking that end they are undone. But what of the First Part of *Tamburlaine*, a play which, as already argued, must be judged apart from Part II? Does it conform to the pattern of Marlowe's later work or is it exceptional in his work and in the whole range of Elizabethan drama in presenting sympathetically the triumphant progress of a tyrant? The dramatists of that age are not slow to announce their intentions. Shakespeare's Richard III, in an opening soliloquy, tells us: 'I am determinèd to prove a villain.' The equally ambitious and equally villainous Selimus, Soldan of Trebizond, boasts in his opening speech that he is an unscrupulous atheist and does so in elaborate rhyme royals. The audience is never left in doubt. They are prepared from the outset for the inevitable downfall at the end. But in 1 *Tamburlaine* there is no such preparation and no such downfall. It is true that many of Tamburlaine's actions and sentiments, considered apart from the play, would be held up to almost universal detestation by the moralists of Marlowe's century. For example, when at the end of the famous apostrophe to Zenocrate Tamburlaine gives the world to note:

> for all my birth
> That Virtue solely is the sum of glory
> And fashions men with true nobility,

and again that

> . . . Virtue is the fount whence honour springs,
> And they are worthy she investeth kings,

to what sort of virtue does he pin his faith, if not the Italian *virtù*, the power of the human intellect and will, and the full development of that power? And again, when he observes that 'Will and Shall best fitteth Tamburlaine' and 'This is my mind and I will have it so', what is this but Juvenal's 'hoc

volo, sic iubeo, sit pro ratione voluntas', a desperate
motto which, long before Marlowe, Luther had
ascribed to Henry VIII and many a Protestant to
many a Papist, a sentiment which Greene in his
Groatsworth of Wit attached to Machiavelli and by
implication to Marlowe? But the question before us
is not what the moralists of the century thought
about tyrants, but what sort of play Marlowe chose
to write about a tyrant. Whetstone had placed *his*
sympathetic account of Tamburlaine in a perfectly
orthodox framework: there Tamburlaine is God's
instrument for the punishment of sin and dissension.
But the career of Marlowe's Tamburlaine is no
mirror to England and Christendom, no instance
of what may happen if virtue is consumed by envy
or malice and obedience by civil dissension. It is
the absence of any condemnation of tyranny and
aggression except, of course, from the tyrants and
aggressors whom Tamburlaine humbles that is so
striking and indeed in that age unparalleled. Can
we doubt that if the young Shakespeare had chosen
Tamburlaine for his hero, the theme of order and
degree would have been the ground-bass of his
play, as it is of his plays on the English kings?
There is much mention of Tamburlaine as the
scourge and wrath of God in Part II, little in Part I.
In Part I all Marlowe's power goes into this repre-

sentation of a Scythian shepherd who becomes a valiant and invincible prince, a man with a reaching and imaginative mind who achieves his ambition both in love and in honour.

Finally, what of Part II? Here the dramatist's attitude is, to say the least, ambiguous. The hero's fortunes always rising in Part I are bound to fall in Part II, as Death conquers first Zenocrate and in the end himself. In Part I Tamburlaine is wholly the centre of interest, his cause uniformly successful, the fine speeches all his, his all the power and all the glory. In Part II, as we have seen, much of the interest is directed elsewhere, especially in the first half of the play; and after the death of Zenocrate, when the fury of his fit is upon him, he becomes a monster of cruelty. Now in this fury he identifies himself with 'The power of heaven's eternal majesty', and allusions to him as the scourge of God, the wrath and terror of the world, come fast and frequent. There is a grim episode in the Tamburlaine story which Marlowe does not use, though it is dramatic enough. Here is Whetstone's version. A merchant of Genoa who frequented Tamburlaine's camp, pitying the women and children trampled to death at his command,

boldly demanded why he shewed such cruelty . . . whom Tamburlaine (with a countenance fired with fury) answered: 'thou supposest that I am a man, but thou art deceived, for I am no other than the ire of God, and the destruction of the world: and therefore see thou come no more in my sight, lest I chasten thy overproud boldness.' The merchant made speed away, and was never afterwards seen in the camp.

That Tamburlaine we see in the third and fourth acts of Marlowe's second part, when his madness is upon him. But in the last scene the fit of fury abates after the potion of his physicians and his last great victory, and he makes his preparations for death. The necessity of death he had accepted at the beginning of Part I when he plighted troth with Theridamas:

> Thus shall my heart be still combined with thine,
> Until our bodies turn to elements:
> And both our souls aspire celestial thrones.

At the height of his fury after the death of Zenocrate, when he is 'Raving, impatient, desperate and mad', he dares the gods out of heaven; but the fury abated he submits to

> those powers
> That mean t' invest me in a higher throne,
> As much too high for this disdainful earth.

It is a double immortality which he promises himself, in the next world, and through his sons

in this world. The last words are with his son:
fire was the element in which Tamburlaine lived,
and now

> earth hath spent the pride of all her fruit,
> And heaven consum'd his choicest living fire.
> Let earth and heaven his timeless death deplore,
> For both their worths will equal him no more.

In all this there is no irony. There is much in
the chronicles and contemporary comment about
the unworthiness of Tamburlaine's sons and the
rapid dissolution of his empire after his death. 'Who
mourns not to hear the two sons of Tamburlaine
more inferior to the meanest than he was superior
to the best?' But of this there is no hint in the play,
only mourning for the loss of a great man, the
extinction of a great force. The theme of Part II is
not, 'What shall it profit a man if he shall gain the
whole world, and lose his own soul?' It is not even
so explicit as 'What shall it profit a man if he shall
gain the whole world and lose his own life?' How far
Marlowe identified himself with the theme which
he presents so powerfully, who can say? He gives
us no chorus, as Jonson might have done. *Sejanus*
has its Arruntius, but not *Tamburlaine*: for Tamburlaine's enemies cannot fill this role; nor his
cowardly son with no thought in his head above a

woman's placket; not even Zenocrate. He fills his
two plays abundantly with passionate life and
thought and it is left to his audience—and his
critics—to make their choice. They may applaud
his hero's fortunes as they please.

III

THE JEW OF MALTA
DOCTOR FAUSTUS

IN my last lecture I quoted the saying of Charles
Lamb that Marlowe's works were all of a different kind. If, as seems likely, *The Jew of Malta* was
his next play after *Tamburlaine*, the change in his
verse is truly remarkable. Decorum is a great matter, so his century believed; but the decorum of
style which Marlowe observes is something more
vital than a doctrine of the schools consciously and
externally applied: his decorum is not rhetorical,
but poetical, the choice of a great dramatic poet.
In *Tamburlaine* the nature of the theme had led him
to an elevated diction and imagery remote from the
everyday world of man. It is not that the theme is
remote from life, as we in our age have had occasion
to realize, but that the insolence of Tamburlaine's
vaunting verse lays itself open to Ben Jonson's
charge that it 'flies from all humanity'. That charge
is a very natural one for the Jacobean Jonson to
make, with his clear-cut ideas on the nature and
function of dramatic language; but it is not wholly
just. And in a way the charge is also unkind, for
Jonson was biting the hand that fed him. The

creator of those monomaniacs Sejanus, Volpone,
and Sir Epicure Mammon learnt much from Marlowe, though *their* raptures are of earth, not
of fire. But it is true that Jonson had less to
learn from *Tamburlaine* than from *The Jew* and
Doctor Faustus, for more and more Marlowe's poetic
energy is released from the diction of common
life.

Is there another English play before *The Jew of
Malta* which opens in mid-speech? 'So that of thus
much that return was made.' It is Barabas, the rich
Jew of Malta, in his counting-house telling his
heaps of gold and silver, grumbling at the labour,
and wishing the treasure were in wedges of gold
and precious jewels, so enclosing 'Infinite riches in
a little room'. How dramatic is this opening soliloquy of eighty-three lines. The character is doing
something all the time—now counting his money,
now cramming it into his steel-barred coffers, now
scanning the weather-vane in the hope that his
argosies at sea have favourable winds. The movement and the gestures of the actor are suggested in
every line. But the speech is not only dramatic, it
is dramatic poetry: the language and the rhythms
are in vital relationship to the sense. Consider how
the alliteration adds to the scorn of 'Here have I
purst their paltry silverlings.' Consider the placing

of the word 'miracle' after the heavily accented line which leads up to it:

> The needy groom that never finger'd groat
> Would make a miracle of thus much coin.

Consider how the colloquial level of a line like 'Fie; what a trouble 'tis to count this trash!' or 'And for a pound to sweat himself to death' changes with the theme and mood to the melodiously alliterative:

> Mine argosy from Alexandria,
> Loaden with spice and silks, now under sail,
> Are smoothly gliding down by Candy shore
> To Malta, through our Mediterranean sea.

As for variation of pace, consider in the following lines how the actor's voice is compelled to linger as Barabas gloats over the names of precious stones, then to hurry on to the climax:

> Bags of fiery Opals, Sapphires, Amethysts,
> Jacinths, hard Topaz, grass-green Emeralds,
> Beauteous Rubies, sparkling Diamonds,
> And seld-seen costly stones of so great price,
> As one of them, indifferently rated,
> And of a caract of this quantity,
> May serve, in peril of calamity,
> To ransom great Kings from captivity.

In this supple and subtle verse, so much can poetry do in a little room, the character of Barabas is laid bare.

The momentum of the verse is notable. In the passage just quoted, while the voice must always pause at the end of a line, the rhythm urges the speaker on to the end of the sense-unit. And there is another innovation in Marlowe's verse, as remarkable historically as the way the ardour and resonance of his lines build themselves into a paragraph, an innovation absent from *Tamburlaine* and more noticeable in *The Jew* than in any play of his except *Doctor Faustus*; I mean the use of a strong pause within the line. As towards the end of this soliloquy at the opening of Act II when Barabas waits beneath his daughter Abigail's window for the treasure she is to throw down to him:

> Thus, like the sad presaging Raven that tolls
> The sick man's passport in her hollow beak,
> And in the shadow of the silent night
> Doth shake contagion from her sable wings;
> Vex'd and tormented runs poor Barabas
> With fatal curses towards these Christians.
> The incertain pleasures of swift-footed time
> Have ta'en their flight, and left me in despair;
> And of my former riches rests no more
> But bare remembrance; like a soldier's scar
> That has no further comfort for his maim.
> O Thou that with a fiery pillar led'st
> The sons of Israel through the dismal shades,
> Light Abraham's offspring; and direct the hand

Of Abigail this night; or let the day
Turn to eternal darkness after this:
No sleep can fasten on my watchful eyes,
Nor quiet enter my distemper'd thoughts,
Till I have answer of my Abigail.

But there is more to be admired in this speech than the architecture of the verse. The stage-direction before the speech is merely 'Enter Barabas with a light'. The light tells the audience the time of day before the actor has spoken, but as he speaks the audience forget taper and daylight alike as it comes under the spell of the poet's words; and it is compelled to do this by the phrasing, the sense of musical delight which, as Coleridge observed in one of his brilliant *aperçus*, is also a gift of imagination. Many an innovation had yet to be introduced into dramatic blank verse during the generation after Marlowe before the medium became used up and incapable of great dramatic verse; but a dramatic poet who can write as Marlowe does in these first two acts is no Moses standing on the border 'of the blest promis'd Land'; the 'barren wilderness' is passed.

The character which he portrays is, as is usual with him, that of a man of exceptional power seeking exceptional power. This is no conventional stage-miser, no monster of a Jew. Like Tamburlaine he has a reaching and imaginative mind, but a mind that turns to wealth, not to empire:

> A reaching thought will search his deepest wits
> And cast with cunning for the time to come.

Like Volpone, he values wealth not merely for its own sake but as the sinews of power and for the assurance it gives that he is 'fram'd of finer mould than common men'. Like Shylock, he divides his allegiance between three ruling passions, himself, his gold, and his daughter. Despising the Christians and their 'malice, falsehood, and excessive pride', he is content to pursue his unmolested way. But when his wealth is confiscated with every circumstance of sanctimonious hypocrisy, hatred turns to a violent passion for revenge. Machiavel, the English Machiavel, justly appears as Prologue to the play, for he is the presiding genius over Jew and Christian alike. Whether Marlowe had read Machiavelli is doubtful: in any case, the only Machiavelli whom a popular audience would have understood or tolerated was the English Machiavel, he that 'weighs not men, and therefore not men's words'. So the Jew in soliloquy:

> I am not of the tribe of Levi, I,
> That can so soon forget an injury.
> We Jews can fawn like spaniels when we please;

> And when we grin we bite; yet are our looks
> As innocent and harmless as a lamb's.
> I learnt in Florence how to kiss my hand,
> Heave up my shoulders when they call me dog,
> And duck as low as any bare-foot friar;
> Hoping to see them starve upon a stall.

In pursuit of his revenge he takes in service the Turkish slave, Ithamore, tests his inclinations in that speech of glorious rodomontade which begins:

> As for myself, I walk abroad a nights
> And kill sick people groaning under walls:
> Sometimes I go about and poison wells; . . .

and when Ithamore has replied in the same vein he is accepted as a junior partner in villainy. The Jew's hatred is directed above all at the Governor of Malta, Ferneze, and before the second act closes he has set at enmity his daughter's two lovers, one of them the Governor's son, and has forged a challenge to a duel.

So the first two acts, and they are the work of genius. In the last three, genius has almost disappeared and except for a few passages here and there so too has talent. There is little in the first two acts that could have been written by any other man: in the last three there is very little that could not have come from the pen of another writer—and a small writer at that. We may concede that a genius—Shakespeare as well as Marlowe—often writes below his form, but even the defects of his bad work betray signs of his good. In the last three acts of *The Jew* there are not many signs that Marlowe is at work. The discrepancy is so great that one would welcome evidence that the players lost the manuscript of the last three acts and had to reconstruct them as best they could.

The weakness is most apparent in the fourth act. The first three scenes (in verse) are given over to the rivalry between two friars for Barabas's wealth, the strangling of one of them by Barabas and his slave, Ithamore, and the trick by which the second friar is persuaded that he is responsible for his brother friar's death. The last three scenes (in prose) are devoted to the infatuation of Ithamore for Bellamira, a courtesan (a theme introduced in the first scene of the third act), her pickpurse bully, Pilia-Borza, acting as intermediary between the Turk and his master. The tone of the whole act is comic or farcical, with only occasional touches of savage humour. The dramatist's grip over his material is relaxed, and the tragic tension so magnificently sustained in Acts I and II is dissipated by the intermediary scenes.

But this is not all. In the five scenes of the first two acts there are almost as many lines as in the sixteen short scenes of the last three acts. In the six scenes of the fourth act and the five scenes of the last act there is little room for anything but farce or the rudiments of plot. The verse for the most part is flat and conventional, and could have come from a man who did little more than add line to line with the sole idea of continuing the action. What is most serious is that there is no room for those long speeches—the special glory of the first two acts and of Marlowe's other plays— which reveal character and strike to the core of the play's intention.

To suppose that the same man who wrote the first two acts was wholly responsible for the last three is revolting to sense and sensibility, for these belong to a different world of art, if indeed they can be said to belong to the world of art at all. We may dismiss the view that Marlowe accommodated his style to the villainy of his subject. If a poet takes chaos as his theme, he does not find it necessary to make his form chaotic. This would be decorum with a vengeance. When in *The Mirror for Magistrates* a member of the company objects to the halting metre of the poem on Richard III, he is answered that '*decorum*, is specially to be observed in all things. Seeing, then, that King Richard never kept measure in any of his doings, seeing also he speaketh in Hell, whereas is no order: it were against the *decorum* of his personage, to use either good metre or order.' To this we need not look for a worthier answer than is provided by Thomas Fuller: 'Hell itself would be wholly confounded, if some superiority were not observed.'

What of the view that Marlowe tired of the play after the second act and abandoned it to unworthy hands? In rejecting this view I am fortified by the opinion of the editor of this play, Mr. H. S. Bennett. We should have to suppose that in writing a play Marlowe began at the beginning and wrote steadily on. Lope de Vega may have worked on this plan: he observed that one act occupies one sheet (sixteen leaves), and four acts make a *comedia*: but system was essential to a man who was to write 1,800 plays. If we watch Marlowe at work in *Doctor Faustus* we find him writing those scenes or speeches which caught his interest, whether in the first act or the last, and leaving the interstices to a collaborator. Another objection to this view is that infrequent as the traces of Marlowe are in the last three acts, yet there *are* traces of him.

We read *The Jew of Malta* in a text which was not printed till 1633. In that year it was the property of Queen Henrietta's men, and the printed edition contains the prologues to their performances at Court and at the Cockpit, and a dedicatory preface by their leading actor–dramatist, Thomas Heywood. In the forty years since Marlowe's death some amplification of the comic scenes, some shortening and degradation of the serious scenes were to be expected. The sensational nature of the play encouraged disintegration, for we learn, and we are not surprised to learn, that it was among those plays which were in demand at Shrovetide, when the players were forced to act what their rowdy audience demanded if they wished to prevent a riot and save the fabric of their theatre. Heywood himself has been suspected of assisting in the contamination of the play, and it has been noted that he twice used the story of the rival friars. The wonder is not that so little of Marlowe's work should have survived in the last three acts but that the first two acts should have been preserved to us almost intact.

But it may be objected that even if we allow that Marlowe's lines were cut to pieces, such a plot could hardly have resulted in anything but crude melodrama. The original design must always have shown how Abigail's lovers were betrayed into their duel and their death by Barabas, how Abigail in detestation of her father's crimes went over to the Christians and (unlike Jessica) suffered death at the hands of a father fearful that she would betray him, how the Jew betrayed Malta to the besieging Turks, and then proposed to betray the Turks to the Christians, how he overreached himself in the end and was boiled in his own cauldron. (The Jew's cauldron is mentioned among the properties of the Admiral's men in an inventory dated March 1598.) The same objection might be taken to *Hamlet* by anyone who knew the plot without knowing the play. In *The Jew* that 'terribly serious, even savage comic humour', so absent (*pace* Mr. T. S. Eliot) from the last act, so present in the first two acts, might if continued have given power and significance even to villainy so sensational. Had the play continued on the same high level, it might have been an indictment of the cruelty and inhumanity of man. It might have shown Marlowe stripping the ragged vices of all time naked as at their birth, or—to borrow the words which Mr. Eliot uses of Machiavelli—it might have shown Marlowe blowing the gaff on human nature.

The Jew of Malta is the only play of Marlowe's the plot of which has not been traced to its source. Is it that unusual thing, an Elizabethan play with an invented plot? For *Doctor Faustus*, Marlowe and his collaborator went to the English translation of the German 'Faust-Book', *The History of the damnable*

life and deserved death of Doctor John Faustus. In
spite of the seriousness of the subject, this compila-
tion resembles in many ways those jest-biographies
which were imported from the folk-literature of
Germany and the Low Countries. Some of these
German folk-heroes had been introduced to English
readers in the late fifteenth and the early sixteenth
centuries: the foul boor Markolf, the ingenious and
facetious parson of Kalenberg, and that gross mocker
and deceiver Howleglass, who is Ulenspiegel. They
are among the books which in their day were read
by all but scholars, and in our day are read by none
but scholars. The humour of these practical jokers
is for the most part scatologic. 'We could not read
Ulenspiegel', writes C. H. Herford, 'but for the
light which it throws upon a society which could
and did.' We could not read the greater part of *The
Damnable Life* but for the light which it throws
upon the play. In the pamphlet Faustus the magi-
cian is also Faustus the practical joker. Most of the
trivialities upon which Faustus spends himself between his damnation and his death are brought into
the play from the source. Marlowe's collaborator
invented almost nothing except the dialogue. There
in the pamphlet he found the jests about the Pope's
buffet, the courtier's horns, the horse-corser who
pulled Faustus's leg from his body, the forty-dollar

horse that vanished when ridden into the water, the consumption of the load of hay. And for the anti-Pope theme he went to Foxe's Book of Martyrs. I say Marlowe's collaborator, for the conclusion is inescapable that Marlowe's hand is nowhere to be found in these scenes. It is also to be said that these scenes formed a part of the original play. The collaborator served his company better than he served posterity. We may say of his scenes, as Falstaff says of his conscripts: 'They'll fill a pit as well as better.' Marlowe must have known how ill these ephemera sorted with those scenes in which he moves pity and terror as they had never been moved before upon the English stage.

Our knowledge of the text of *Doctor Faustus* has been greatly enriched by Sir Walter Greg's parallel-text edition of the two substantive texts—the editions of 1604 and 1616. Outside Shakespeare there is no play the textual problems of which are more complex and (by reason of the greatness of the material) more rewarding of study; and Greg's solution of these problems is indispensable to the critic. In this very brief summary of his conclusions, he allows me to use here and there his own words.

The play was written by Marlowe in collaboration with at least one other playwright. The text printed in 1604 is a 'bad' quarto, representing a

reconstruction from memory not of the piece as
originally performed in 1592 or 1593, but of that
piece shortened for provincial acting, occasionally
interpolated, and the clowning parts expanded to
suit the taste of a vulgar audience and the taste and
capacity of a declining company of players. It pre-
serves, however, almost all Marlowe's share in the
composition, and presents it with substantial fidel-
ity, though far from verbal accuracy. The text of
1616 was prepared for publication by an editor on
the basis of a manuscript containing the drafts of
the authors, i.e. their 'foul papers', those very drafts
from which the original prompt-book was tran-
scribed. Some of the differences between the two
texts, however, are to be explained by a revision
which took place after the authors had handed in
their drafts and while the prompt-book was being
prepared, a revision which found its way, of course,
into the stage version that underlies the text of
1604.

If this were the whole story, the textual history
of the play would be comparatively simple: we
should have a good quarto printed from the authors'
manuscripts, and we should have a bad quarto the
value of which would reside in the information it
gave us of the revision which the play underwent
as it was being prepared for the stage and in the

authentic news it supplied in its stage directions of the way the play was produced, not on the London stage but under the primitive conditions of a small travelling company acting in the provinces. The position would be rather like that of *Hamlet* if the Folio text based upon the prompt-copy had perished: for there too we have a bad quarto, though a bad quarto a good deal worse than the bad quarto of *Doctor Faustus*, and there too we have a good quarto printed from the author's drafts. On occasions, however, the printer of the good quarto of *Hamlet* consulted the bad quarto, and so here and there gave us a contaminated text. In *Doctor Faustus* this sort of contamination is much more serious. In the twenty-four years which had elapsed since Marlowe and his collaborator wrote their play, their 'foul papers' had become incomplete and in parts damaged or illegible, so that the editor of the 1616 text was sometimes forced to reproduce passages from the text of 1604, a copy of the third edition of which (1611) he had at hand—forced to reproduce these passages either as they stood in the bad quarto or with such corrections as could be deciphered in the manuscript. From the text of 1611 the editor also took over some of the prompt-book revisions and even some of the interpolations from this imperfect report of an acting version. Finally, this editor of 1616 made a number of cuts and alterations of his own, mostly on the score of profanity, but a few on literary grounds.

One more problem may be briefly discussed: how far had the text reported in the 'bad' quarto already suffered from interpolation or revision? We know from Henslowe's Diary that in 1602 Birde and Rowley were paid the substantial sum of £4 for writing additions to the play, and if we had to suppose that the 'bad' quarto was based on an acting version which already included these additions, its value as evidence of the original stage version would be greatly reduced. But Greg has shown that the only passage in the bad quarto which must be later than 1592 or 1593 is a bit of gag in the episode of the horse-corser with its reference to Dr. Lopez, whose trial and execution took place in 1594: and other evidence points to the conclusion that the bad text which got into print in 1604 was assembled not later than 1594 or thereabouts.

As we consider the texts in which we have to read much of our Marlowe, we are helped to realize our good fortune that the company in which Shakespeare was both shareholder and householder and for which he wrote his plays was the most stable and most prosperous in that age, that his plays were put into print some of them during his lifetime

and all of them soon after his death, and that
their publication was undertaken by two of his
friends. Marlowe's memory and fame were not
cherished in this way, yet the result of Greg's
investigation is to show that the text of *Doctor
Faustus* is not so desperately corrupt as has been
usually held. While it would be folly to suppose
that we have as good a text of the play as we have
of *Hamlet*, we may believe that Marlowe's share
in the play has survived with little injury and that
the conjectural reconstruction which Greg has published separately resembles pretty closely the play
which Marlowe and his collaborator wrote.

If we believe, then, that *Doctor Faustus* begins
and ends magnificently, but that this magnificence
is dissipated by the comic and the farcical scenes—
the distinction between what is comic and what is
farcical is, as Greg allows, hardly perceptible—and
by the trivial uses to which Faustus puts the power
which he is given at so terrible a price, we must
also believe that the blame rests not with any de-
graders or interpolators but with the original itself.
The middle of the play always was disfigured by
comic and clownish scenes not only feeble in invention but grossly out of harmony with the tragic
theme. The collaborator was a hackwriter, possibly
also an actor, more closely in touch with the life of

the theatre than Marlowe and much nearer the mental level and dramatic taste of the actors. We may see how little Marlowe had to do with the central scenes if we look for his work between the show of the Seven Deadly Sins in II. ii and the last scene of all, v. ii: his hand may be detected only in the description of Italy and Rome in III. i (forty lines) and in the first and second appearances of Helen in v. i (some forty-seven lines). What should we say of a play of Shakespeare's which contained but eighty-seven lines from his pen in the twelve scenes between Act II, Scene ii and the last scene of the last act? Even in the scenes which are mainly of Marlowe's composition the weak hand of the collaborator is sometimes visible, as in the dialogue between the Good and Bad Angels in the last scene, written in a vein of sentimental piety quite alien to Marlowe's genius.

Yet these considerations may rather enhance than diminish our sense of Marlowe's greatness as a dramatic poet. Here is a play in which not more than 825 lines can be attributed to his hand, and those clustered together for the most part in the opening and closing scenes. How the play was planned—whether Marlowe took the share that interested him and of free will abandoned the rest to the mercy of his collaborator, or whether the players insisted on the incorporation of the comic and farcical incidents in the *Damnable Life*—there is no knowing. Only on the naïve principle of decorum which I have already mentioned can we suppose that Marlowe intended the lapse into buffoonery as a symptom of Faustus's betrayal of his ideals and of a gradual deterioration in character. Yet if we avert our eyes from the collaborator's work and look only at Marlowe's, we may yet say, with Goethe, 'How greatly is it all planned'—and executed, too. If we may judge from the few contemporary references, the play owed its success upon the stage to spectacle and clowning; to the 'dragon' which appears in 1598 among the properties of the Admiral's men; to the shag-haired devils who ran roaring over the stage with squibs in their mouths when Faustus went to the devil, while the drummers made thunders in the tiring-house and the twelvepenny hirelings an artificial lightning in the heavens. The sensationalism of the plot and the production gave rise to the story, vouched for by Prynne and others, that at one performance the actors were disconcerted by the discovery that 'there was one devil too many amongst them' and contrary to their usual custom spent the rest of the night in reading and in prayer. Marlowe's imagination transcends this simple and crude story of a man who sold his soul to the devil and raises the theme to a lofty plane of spiritual insight. Whatever his views on religion may have been, in this play he was absorbed by his theme and wrote as one possessed.

Many a preacher of the day had warned his congregation of the desperate catastrophe of those who cut themselves off from the mercy of God by 'presumptuous, aspiring, heaven-daring sins' and had preached that 'as faith is heaven before heaven, so despair is damnation before the time'. And once before Marlowe an Englishman had cast into dramatic form the theme of a man who denied God and fell into despair. He too was from Corpus. Marlowe may never have seen Nathaniel Woodes's *Conflict of Conscience*, and if he had he could have felt nothing but contempt for this Norwich minister's clumsy rhyme royals and fourteeners: but he must have heard of the case which gave Woodes his theme, for it was in his age and for generations to come a famous Protestant *exemplum*. Woodes's source was an English translation of part of a Latin account, introduced by John Calvin, of how a wealthy Italian lawyer, Francesco Spira, recanted from the Protestant faith in order to save his life and property, believed that he had committed the sin against the Holy Ghost, and fell into final and total despair.

Interviewed by his friends and spiritual advisers he told them that he was already in hell, in continual torment, that while the mercy of God far surmounted all the sins of the world it could avail him nothing, for he was neither elected nor in God's favour, but had been always reprobate and cursed from the beginning; that pardon was no more possible to him than to take the whole water of the sea in one spoon and drink it up at a draught; that he longed for death, wishing to be in the place of Judas or Cain, and to go to hell with all speed, looking every hour for the terrible sentence of God.

In Marlowe's share of the play there is nothing of predestination and reprobation. He concentrates on the human tragedy of Faustus and leaves us in no doubt that Faustus's will was free. If there is one sentence in *The Damnable Life* which represents without distortion his conception of the theme, it is: 'give none the blame but thine own self-will, thy proud and aspiring mind, which both brought thee into the wrath of God and utter damnation.' There is no hint in his share of the play that the infernal powers plotted his downfall: it is not Marlowe who makes Mephostophilis boast that when Faustus took up Jerome's Bible his eye was directed to the texts which led him to prefer necromancy to divinity: and Greg argues that the stage-direction in

the text of 1616 which introduces Lucifer and four
devils as silent and unobserved witnesses of Faustus's compact with Mephostophilis is an addition
due to the collaborator's different conception of
Faustus's downfall. Marlowe's Faustus makes a
free choice.

> Oh, what a world of profit and delight,
> Of power, of honour, of omnipotence
> Is promis'd to the studious artizan!
> All things that move between the quiet poles
> Shall be at my command: emperors and kings
> Are but obeyed in their several provinces,
> Nor can they raise the wind or rend the clouds;
> But his dominion that exceeds in this
> Stretcheth as far as doth the mind of man:
> A sound magician is a demi-god;
> Here tire my brains to get a deity!

Recent critics have pointed out how Faustus is
cheated by the devil's promises, how he sells eternity for a toy. He asks for a wife, but his request is
evaded, for he can never have a wife. He puts the
question 'Who made the world?' and receives no
answer. 'Villain,' he cries to Mephostophilis, 'have
I not bound thee to tell me any thing'; and is
answered: 'Ay, that is not against our kingdom:
this is. Thou art damned; think thou of hell.' But
there is a more dreadful deceit in the requests which
he *is* granted. Nowhere is this more apparent than in

the two appearances of Helen. Upon these appearances Marlowe lavishes all the magnificence at his
command of richness of association and cadence,
whether at her first appearance—

> No marvel though the angry Greeks pursued
> With ten years' war the rape of such a queen,
> Whose heavenly beauty passeth all compare—

or in the famous apostrophe at her second appearance. But Helen is the anodyne to deaden the
anguish of his fears, and the beauty has a terrible
irony. This is still true even if we do not accept the
view that Helen is a succuba and that in his union
with her Faustus has committed the sin of demonia-
lity and sealed his damnation. If that had been the
dramatists' intention, they would, I think, have
made it more explicit. It is true, however, that
before Faustus's union with Helen the Old Man
does not despair of his salvation and that after it he
does. But the Old Man was taken over from *The
Damnable Life* not by Marlowe but by a collaborator. In Marlowe's share of the play Faustus seals
his damnation when he seals with his blood the
deed by which he gives body and soul to the devil.
Having done that he has become a 'spirit', and
'spirit' in this play always means an evil spirit.
'Thou art a spirit; God cannot pity thee', says the
Bad Angel. Prompted by the Good Angel Faustus

is conscious that even if he is a devil God may yet pity him if he repents; but the Bad Angel has the last word: 'Ay, but Faustus never shall repent'; and Faustus knows this to be true: 'My heart is hardened, I cannot repent.' So with Francis Spira as his story is narrated in the English pamphlet. The spirit of God continually came into his mind, saying: 'Francis, beware . . . thou art free yet, Francis, . . . repent, and God will have mercy upon thee.' But though he believed all that was said it availed him nothing: 'My heart is utterly hardened: Ye labour in vain.' But there is this difference between Spira and Marlowe's sensualist: that Spira fell at once into total and final despair. When his friends asked him what he would do if he had a sword in his hand he replied: 'Give me a sword and ye shall see what I will do . . . I cannot tell . . . neither can I say what my will then should be.' And he took advantage of the earliest opportunity to kill himself. But in the play, when 'guns and knives, Swords, poisons, halters and envenom'd steel' are laid before Faustus, he does not dispatch himself, for 'sweet pleasure' conquers 'deep despair':

> Have not I made blind Homer sing to me
> Of Alexander's love and Oenon's death?
> And hath not he, that built the walls of Thebes
> With ravishing sound of his melodious harp,

Made music with my Mephostophilis?
Why should I die then, or basely despair?
I am resolv'd Faustus shall not repent.

Not until the night has arrived when his soul
is forfeit does he fall into total and final despair.
In this great scene not Marlowe's are the taunts
of Mephostophilis: not Marlowe's are the Good
Angel's conventional picture of the joys of heaven
and still less the Bad Angel's lurid description of
the physical horrors of hell. Here, as Greg main-
tains, it is not so much the 'morality' element as
the human tragedy upon which Marlowe insists.
His share in the scene is in two parts: Faustus's
leavetaking with his friends and his last speech. In
the farewell which Faustus takes with the scholars
we have, Greg observes, probably the only considerable prose passage that Marlowe ever wrote:
'its moral earnestness marks it off from anything
the collaborator was capable of writing.' Is it not
the earliest appearance in our drama of prose that is
passionately serving the purpose of tragedy? In the
maturity of Jacobean tragedy we are prepared for it
—the later Shakespeare or Webster may deviate
into prose without sinking from the high tragic
level; but here is Marlowe doing it as early as
1592 or 1593. We may count that as one more
token of what our drama lost by his early death.

One thing this scene does is to exhibit the affection which the scholars feel for their friend and their concern for his fate: it helps to bring pity to the end as well as terror. Unusually bare of ornament and image, this prose rises above plain exposition as gusts of terror shake Faustus's mind, gusts which find expression in the passionate figure of epizeuxis: whether in Faustus's 'Look sirs! comes he not, comes he not?', as his fears suggest that Mephostophilis has come before his time; or in the cry 'Hell, ah hell for ever! Sweet friends, what shall become of Faustus, being in hell for ever?'; or in his vain attempts to pray, 'I would lift up my hands, but see, they hold 'em, they hold 'em'; or as his friends depart to pray for him, 'Ay, pray for me, pray for me'. The mind thinks forward to still greater contexts in plays yet to be written where this figure of rhetoric is used in passion: 'It is the cause, it is the cause, my soul' or Lear's five-fold 'Never'.

For the text of the last soliloquy, the greatest of many in Marlowe, we have to depend wholly upon the bad quarto. Here and there the line division has gone wrong, but the damage is not serious.

> . . . Why wert thou not a creature wanting soul?
> Or why is this immortal that thou hast?
> Ah, Pythagoras' metempsychosis, were that true,
> This soul should fly from me, and I be changed

> Unto some brutish beast. All beasts are happy,
> For when they die,
> Their souls are soon dissolv'd in elements;
> But mine must live still to be plagu'd in hell . . .

The same desire was to come into the tortured mind of John Bunyan before he was cured of his despair and went home rejoicing: 'The beasts, birds, fishes, &c. I blessed their condition; for they had not a sinful nature, they were not obnoxious to the wrath of God, they were not to go to Hell-fire after death.' It is one of many vain desires that flash into Faustus's mind, as he twists and turns to escape his fate, as time passes inexorably into eternity. Sometimes, as here, the sense unit extends over a number of lines: and sometimes the agony of the speaker breaks it more than once within the line or into a half line. These broken rhythms are surely Marlowe's, not the reporter's, and more evidence of how far he had travelled since *Tamburlaine*. Echoes from earlier work are exalted as they become knit into this great context: Tamburlaine's 'And set black streamers in the firmament' is exalted into 'See, see, where Christ's blood streams in the firmament'; Edward II's prayer to the sun to 'continue ever'—-

> Stand still, you watches of the element,
> All times and seasons rest you at a stay,—

into Faustus's

> Stand still, you ever-moving spheres of heaven,
> That time may cease, and midnight never come;

and Dido's 'as many. . . . As in the sea are little water drops' into

> O soul, be chang'd to little water drops,
> And fall into the ocean, ne'er be found.

Strangest exaltation of all is that line adapted from Ovid's *Amores*, translated by the poet in his Cambridge days, which now becomes the agonized cry of Faustus cut off from God and man: *O lente lente currite noctis equi.*

The play over, there follows the Chorus. If it is Marlowe's, and it may well be his, it is Marlowe deliberately underwriting, to give a quiet and solemn ending in formalized verse. No moral can represent the experience which the play has given, but convention demanded a moral, and one is supplied:

Cut is the branch that might have grown full straight,
And burnèd is Apollo's laurel bough
That sometime grew within this learnèd man.
Faustus is gone: regard his hellish fall,
Whose fiendful fortune may exhort the wise
Only to wonder at unlawful things,
Whose deepness doth entice such forward wits
To practise more than heavenly power permits.

IV

THE MASSACRE AT PARIS
EDWARD II

EDWARD II is the one play of Marlowe's—except *Dido*—which is not dominated by one character, and that a character with an aspiring mind: for the centre of this play is not Mortimer but Edward. Some have held that the reason for this change lies in the fact that Marlowe wrote *Edward II* for another dramatic company, not for the Admiral's men with the famous Edward Alleyn who distinguished himself in the parts of Tamburlaine, Barabas, and Faustus, but for Pembroke's men who were without an Alleyn. But the history and personnel of Pembroke's company in the plague years of 1592–3, when we first hear of them, is obscure: in those bad times for actors, companies broke up and re-formed in bewildering fashion. In this Serbonian bog of Elizabethan theatrical history I do not venture to tread, yet I must say that I find unconvincing the view that Marlowe changed his theme to suit his actors; for there never has been a company of professional actors which did not contain at least two men who thought themselves capable of playing star parts of the greatest magnitude. As probably, Marlowe may have been influenced by the success of Shakespeare's *Henry VI*, where the dramatic interest is spread over a yet wider range of characters.

But there is another chronicle play of Marlowe's about which a word or two may be said first. If *The Massacre at Paris* had survived as Marlowe wrote it, much more than a word or two would be necessary. It is our misfortune that the text is a reported text so maimed in the reporting that criticism can only guess at Marlowe's intention and achievement. Some 1,250 lines of verse are all that have survived, and some of these are not garbled versions of Marlowe's lines but half remembered echoes from other plays with which the reporter has patched them up. The dialogue is stripped almost to the bare bones of the action.

The historical period covered is the murder of Coligny and the night of St. Bartholomew in 1572, the murder of Guise in 1588, the murder of Henry III and the accession of Henry of Navarre in 1589. Marlowe's play is then a chronicle play, presenting upon the stage the sensational news 'de furoribus Gallicis' which had been reported in England in many a pamphlet and ballad. The play was written before Henry IV had decided that Paris was worth a mass; hence he could be presented as the champion of the Protestant cause against the Machiavellian policies of the Guise faction, the weakness of Charles IX dominated by his mother Catherine de Medici, and his equally weak brother Henry III whose mind, like Edward II's,

> runs on his minions
> And all his heaven is to delight himself.

Perhaps we may most regret the reporter's ineptitude in the scene which represents the murder of the Duke of Guise. The historical evidence has survived in a form which is already dramatic, and not the less vivid in our minds for memories of the setting in the royal castle at Blois and of the rooms where the king and his guards waited for the murdered man. There is quality too in the words which history has recorded as passing between Henry III and his mother. His words to her after the murder 'Je suis seul roi maintenant' are preserved in the play in a line which is too good to have come from a reporter: 'I ne'er was king of France until this hour'; but the irony of the words—for that was exactly what Henry was not—is but dimly discerned in the text that has survived. And we look in vain for that enigmatic remark of the king as he spurned with his foot the body of the Guise: 'Il paraît encore plus grand que vivant.' It is one of those instinctive reflections which while they may come from the top layer of the mind yet illuminate at deeper levels the speaker and the situation. One might say that it was only waiting for a great context in order to become art: then, it might have been signed by Middleton or Webster.

We cannot doubt that it was the towering ambition of Guise that most attracted Marlowe to this theme. One soliloquy of his, and only one, has survived, we may suppose, in something like the form that Marlowe gave it: significantly, it is nearly three times longer than any other speech in the play. Like the opening soliloquy in *Richard III* it is a proud confession of faith, the speech of a man 'determinèd to prove a villain'. In this speech Guise's character is fixed and determinate, as was Richard's. There can be no surprises except surprises of situation. It is the character of a man who uses religion as a stalking-horse, and the game which he shoots at is absolute power, the crown of France. As with Marlowe's other studies in ambition he has a mastering intellect, though overreached in the end, and danger is the element in which he lives and thrives, 'the chiefest way to happiness':

> What glory is there in a common good,
> That hangs for every peasant to achieve?

That like I best, that flies beyond my reach.
Set me to scale the high Pyramides,
And thereon set the Diadem of France;
I'll either rend it with my nails to naught,
Or mount the top with my aspiring wings,
Although my downfall be the deepest hell.
For this I wake, when others think I sleep,
For this I wait, that scorns attendance else;
For this, my quenchless thirst, whereon I build,
Hath often pleaded kindred to the King;
For this, this head, this heart, this hand and sword,
Contrives, imagines, and fully executes,
Matters of import aimèd at by many,
Yet understood by none.

If there was ambiguity in the presentation of Tamburlaine, there is none here. Poison, murder, and massacre are the steps by which Guise mounts the ladder of his ambition, but when the crown seems within his grasp he is outwitted by the man he had despised. In watching this play the orthodox could settle comfortably in their places to watch the downfall of a man who was at once a Frenchman, a Papist, an Atheist, and a King-queller.

The Massacre at Paris is exceptional among the plays of that date in being based on contemporary European history. It is a kind of plot which Shakespeare did not touch. In *Edward II* Marlowe is following the example which Shakespeare had already set: he goes to the English chronicles. Anyone who doubts whether Marlowe's gifts were really dramatic would do well to read Holinshed's account of the reign of Edward II and see with what art of selection, condensation, and adaptation Marlowe has shaped out of the chronicle history of a disagreeable reign an historical tragedy. The title suggests a chronicle: 'The troublesome reign and lamentable death of Edward the Second, King of England: with the tragical fall of proud Mortimer'; but although history, especially in Acts II and III, is not wholly assimilated into drama, the running-title 'The Tragedy of Edward the Second' represents the play better. Marlowe did not read so widely in the histories as did Michael Drayton for the 'Complaint' of Piers Gaveston written in the year of Marlowe's death, but he was not satisfied merely with Holinshed, and went elsewhere for many a detail: for example, the 'fleering' song with which the Scots mocked the English disgrace at Bannockburn, with its refrains 'With a heave and a ho', 'With a rombelow'. And he threw aside as unsuitable to his purposes much material connected with the wars with Scotland and Ireland and France, many a private war between baron and baron, and of course all those trivial disconnected details which the chronicles recorded. Moreover, historical dating and historical sequence he regarded as wholly within his control if it led to economy and coherence, above all if it led to the balance of dramatic power.

The balance of one character or motive with another is here essential, for this is his one play in which his purpose is to illuminate weakness, not strength. Weakness does not act but is acted upon, or if it acts its actions are frustrated and ineffective. Therefore Marlowe was forced by the nature of his theme to distribute the interest over a variety of characters as he never had occasion to do elsewhere, to exhibit not only the central figure of Edward in whom the play's intention is chiefly expressed but also the agents of power and corruption who act upon this figure. The stage is set for the conflict to follow in the four movements of the first scene. First, Gaveston just returned from banishment and eager to meet the King and to devise the sensuous pleasures which delight them both, a Gaveston who is not the mere self-seeker of the chronicles but as much infatuated with the King as the King with him, both men with a 'ruling desire' which counts the world well lost for love and pleasure. Secondly, the King's quarrel with the lords bitterly jealous of the upstart Gaveston, a quarrel overheard by Gaveston, a movement in which we meet the King's chief enemies, Lancaster, both Mortimers, and Warwick. Thirdly, the reunion of Edward and Gaveston. We are used in Shakespeare to the image of sea or river overflowing the land, as a symbol of chaos, an inversion of nature which is a token of evil in human nature; now the image is from Edward himself and marks the absence of all sense of kingly duty and moral scruple:

> I have my wish, in that I joy thy sight;
> And sooner shall the sea o'erwhelm my land,
> Than bear the ship that shall transport thee hence.

In a brief fourth movement Edward and Gaveston violently abuse the Bishop of Coventry and add to the hostility of the lords the powerful hostility of the Church. And so in the first scene, with great economy and power, Marlowe has introduced all the leading characters which are the necessary embodiments of his dramatic purpose except Queen Isabel: and she appears in the second scene. Of these characters Gaveston is murdered at the beginning of the third act; Lancaster is captured at the battle of Boroughbridge at the end of the third act; Mortimer and Isabel alone are as important in the last act as in the first; as the play proceeds their share in the personal tragedy of the King becomes increasingly important.

The part played by one character is too important to omit even in the briefest summary. Though of subsidiary importance the King's brother Edmund Earl of Kent fulfils a function in this play to which I think there is no parallel in Marlowe's other plays. Kent throws in his lot now with the King now with the King's enemies in a vain attempt to trim the ship of state. He is the one character in the play upon whom the affections can rest, the one character—apart from the young Prince Edward—whose concern for the King is wholly untouched by jealousy, hatred, lust, or self-aggrandizement. This character is perhaps the only character in Marlowe's plays who may be regarded as a point of reference.

The similarity between the theme of *Edward II* and that of *Richard II*, written a few years later, is obvious: it must have been obvious to Shakespeare: he certainly knew Marlowe's play and he may have known it the better from having acted in it. In both characters there is fundamental weakness. It is not that there is a chink in their armour: they have no armour at all. In both characters there is change, but the change is not so much in them as in our feelings to them, as we see them passing from the cruelty and selfishness of power to the helplessness and suffering of powerlessness. But the similarities between these two plays are superficial. It is an altogether grimmer world into which Marlowe takes us, a world of evil and corruption

deeper and darker than that of *Richard II*. The
turning-point of Edward's fortunes comes with the
death of Gaveston. Temporarily his fortunes re-
cover with the victory at Boroughbridge, but the
beginning of his end is the escape of Mortimer to
France, whither the Queen and the young Edward
have already been sent. Act IV shows Edward's
defeat and capture by the forces led by Mortimer
and Isabel.

The critics have attacked Marlowe for inconsistency in his portrayal of Mortimer and Isabel, but
is there more inconsistency than dramatic poetry
may claim? There is change, certainly, rather than
development, but which dramatist of this date
attempted to show development? And how very
few attempted to show it later! We must not ask
of an Elizabethan play what we ask of a naturalistic
play. The change in Mortimer's character and in
Isabel's is to add pity and terror to Edward's end,
to assist in the swing from detestation and contempt of Edward when abusing his power to pity
for Edward when he has fallen from high estate.
Until the fourth act Mortimer is hardly distinguish-
able from the other proud and self-seeking lords:
but as soon as Edward is defeated and the power
falls into his own hands he becomes a Machiavel.
'Fear'd am I more than lov'd', and one of the

maxims attributed to Machiavelli was that 'it is better for a Prince to be feared than loved'. Another maxim was that 'A man is happy so long as Fortune agreeth unto his nature and humour', and it is Mortimer and Mortimer alone who calls upon Fortune. At the height of his power he boasts that he makes Fortune's wheel turn as he pleases, and quotes from Ovid the line *Major sum quam cui possit fortuna nocere*. And when Edward's murder is brought home to him, and he sees that his end is in sight, there is no moral compunction but mere acquiescence in the decree of an arbitrary fate.

> Base Fortune, now I see, that in thy wheel
> There is a point, to which when men aspire,
> They tumble headlong down: that point I touch'd,
> And, seeing there was no place to mount up higher,
> Why should I grieve at my declining fall?
> Farewell, fair Queen: weep not for Mortimer,
> That scorns the world, and as a traveller
> Goes to discover countries yet unknown.

But it is the character of Edward's Queen Isabel that has proved the greatest stumbling-block to critics. Yet here again if we remember Marlowe's dramatic purpose and do not seek for realism, we shall find that he has not bungled a matter vital to the balance of his play, just as he made no mistake in departing from the chronicles which make no mention of an intrigue between Isabel and Mortimer before Edward's murder. Of this intrigue we hear much in the first two acts, but always from Edward and Gaveston. They are not to be believed, and the effect of these slanders on the King's neglected Queen is to light up his unhallowed passion for his favourite, his privado.

> Like frantic Juno will I fill the earth
> With ghastly murmur of my sighs and cries;
> For never doted Jove on Ganymede
> So much as he on cursed Gaveston.

This the Queen speaks in soliloquy, and by the conventions of Elizabethan drama we are to suppose her speaking her inmost thoughts. Not until after repeated failures to win the affection of her husband, not until after her question 'No farewell to poor Isabel, thy Queen?' has received the brutal reply 'Yes, yes, for Mortimer, your lover's sake', does she betray the first hint of affection for Mortimer, again in soliloquy:

> So well hast thou deserv'd, sweet Mortimer,
> As Isabel could live with thee for ever.

But not yet has the moment arrived to swing the balance of pity towards Edward, and she continues:

> In vain I look for love at Edward's hand,
> Whose eyes are fix'd on none but Gaveston,
> Yet once more I'll importune him with prayers.

And if prayers fail, she will take refuge with her brother, the King of France. By this soliloquy we are prepared for her guilt, but she is not yet guilty. Marlowe keeps that in reserve until he needs it. And the first assurance of guilt is not given us until she and Mortimer have returned from France with their victorious army. Then this assurance *is* to be believed, for it is given us by Kent, whom I have called Marlowe's point of reference:

> Mortimer
> And Isabel do kiss, while they conspire:
> And yet she bears a face of love forsooth.
> Fie on that love that hatcheth death and hate.

Now Isabel plays she-Machiavel to Mortimer's Machiavel. Cruel as well as unfaithful, she has nothing to learn in the art of turning and dissembling. In public she is full of concern for the state of the country and the King's misfortunes, of thanks to 'the God of kings' and 'heaven's great architect'; in private, there is no villainy of Mortimer's which she does not aid and abet.

It adds to the horror that in the last two acts Edward is never brought face to face with his two tormentors. The fear of their cruelty preys upon his mind in prison, fear as much for his son as for himself, and as in many an age besides Shakespeare's the cruelty of man and woman is expressed in terms of beasts of prey:

> For he's a lamb, encompassèd by wolves,
> Which in a moment will abridge his life.

And again,

> Let not that Mortimer protect my son;
> More safety is there in a tiger's jaws,
> Than his embracements.

The revulsion of feeling from contempt to pity is now complete, and it is in part the change in the characters of Mortimer and Isabel that has effected it.

> What, are you mov'd? pity you me?
> Then send for unrelenting Mortimer,
> And Isabel, whose eyes, being turn'd to steel,
> Will sooner sparkle fire than shed a tear.

At the end Edward is as terrified, as helpless, and as lonely as Faustus. But he is not penitent. Neither is Shakespeare's Richard II. Like Lear these two characters 'did ever slenderly know themselves', and, unlike Lear, they never come to know themselves. The chronicles present us with a penitent Edward, but this was not to Marlowe's purpose. Edward's thoughts are of Mortimer and Isabel, of his own sorrows, his 'guiltless life', his 'innocent hands', and of the safety of his son:

> Commend me to my son, and bid him rule
> Better than I. Yet how have I transgress'd,
> Unless it be with too much clemency?

The humiliation and murder of Edward are narrated in full by the chroniclers. The details are sordid, pitiless, horrible. And Marlowe leaves out little. For one detail which he did not find in Holinshed, the washing and shaving of the King in puddle water, he went to Stow. Compassion did not come easily to Marlowe, and there is a cruelty in these last scenes which we do not find in Shakespeare. In *Richard II* there is every sort of alleviation. Richard is brought face to face with his accusers, and allowed to indulge himself in scenes which make him at once the playboy and the poet of the English kings. He takes affectionate farewell of his Queen—how different an Isabel from Edward's. In place of Mortimer we have a Bolingbroke. And at the end no passive submission, but death in courageous action. Shakespeare's compassion is nowhere more evident than in his invention of the faithful groom of the stable and the talk with his master about 'roan Barbary', when King and groom share a common humanity. In Marlowe there is no groom; instead, the invention of the murderer whom he christens, with a stroke of sardonic humour, Lightborn, the professional murderer who takes a pride in the fine handling of a man. Into his taut tight-lipped lines Marlowe packs the quintessence of all that Englishmen had heard or dreamt of Italianate villainy:

> You shall not need to give instructions;
> 'Tis not the first time I have killed a man.
> I learned in Naples how to poison flowers;
> To strangle with a lawn thrust through the throat;
> To pierce the windpipe with a needle's point;
> Or whilst one is asleep, to take a quill
> And blow a little powder in his ears;
> Or open his mouth and pour quicksilver down.
> But yet I have a braver way than these.

The 'braver way' is reported by the chronicles, but it was too strong even for the stomach of an Elizabethan audience, and the red-hot spit which Lightborn orders to be prepared is not called for. But the wail of the murdered man rang through the theatre, as it did, writes Holinshed,

through the castle and town of Berkeley, so that divers being awakened therewith (as they themselves confessed) prayed heartily to God to receive his soul, when they understood by his cry what the matter meant.

Charles Lamb said that this death-scene moved pity and terror beyond any scene ancient and modern with which he was acquainted. But I wonder if there is not too much horror in the terror, if the scene is not so painful that it presses upon the nerves. In a short last scene Mortimer and Isabel meet their doom, and the young King Edward takes control. In the young Edward's words there is grief for his father and righteous anger with his murderer, but the words rather enforce the feeling that the dramatist does not deeply feel the sacredness of royalty, that the tragedy is in the main a personal tragedy without wider repercussions, and that in the supporting characters he has been exhibiting this and that variety of ambition, hatred, envy, lust, and the corruption of men and women in power or in search of power.

Marlowe's other heroes, except in *Dido* and *The Massacre at Paris*, are men of humble birth: this is his one full study of kingship. He is aware of the irony of kingship, and nowhere in this play is his verse finer and fuller than in the abdication scene. When Shakespeare came to write in *Richard II* of the 'reluctant pangs of abdicating royalty' (the phrase is Lamb's), he remembered the scene, and well he might, for in imagery and in pathos it is nearer to Shakespeare than any other scene in Marlowe. But it stands almost alone in the play as a scene in which Marlowe's poetic power is fully released. When we have admitted that, we have

admitted a weakness which no care for craftsmanship can redeem. Marlowe never returned to the
theme of English history, as Shakespeare did again
and again. He went on to write *Doctor Faustus* and
there he fulfilled himself.

V

MARLOWE AND SHAKESPEARE

WHAT is the relationship of Marlowe's historical play to Shakespeare's earliest historical plays? The old view was that the chronicle play, inspired by the patriotic feeling that swept the country before and after the Armada, was first lifted into the dignity of historical tragedy by Marlowe and that Shakespeare profited from his example in his revision of the two plays which were thought to lie behind *Henry VI*, Parts II and III, and in his *Richard III*. But we now believe that the two quartos printed in 1594 and 1595, *The First Part of the Contention between the two famous Houses of York and Lancaster* and *The True Tragedy of Richard Duke of York*, are not the 'source-plays' of 2 and 3 *Henry VI* but pirated versions of these plays put together by actors relying chiefly upon their memory: and many believe that *Henry VI*, Parts II and III, if not *Henry VI*, Part I, were written by Shakespeare alone and are among his earliest plays. The belief that 2 and 3 *Henry VI* were Shakespeare's revisions of two plays by other men—Marlowe, Greene, Peele, Lodge have all been suspected—was mainly responsible for the view that Shakespeare commenced dramatist as a botcher of other men's plays; but one by one the props for this view have been knocked away.

If 2 and 3 *Henry VI* are Shakespeare's, did they follow or precede *Edward II*? The evidence is well set out by A. P. Rossiter in his edition of *Thomas of Woodstock*, and it suggests that Shakespeare's two history plays are the earlier: for the reason that the two passages in Part II and the one in Part III which resemble passages in *Edward II*, were all three suggested to Shakespeare by the chronicles for the reigns of Henry VI and Edward IV, whereas there are no corresponding passages in the chronicles of Edward II's reign which might have suggested these passages to Marlowe.

Was it Shakespeare and Marlowe who first gave dignity and coherence to the historical play and raised it above the level of a chronicle? So we have always been taught to believe; but when we look for these early chronicle plays written before the Armada, where are they? When Tilburina gave her vivid description of the fight between the Armada and the English fleet, her father rebuked her with the words:

The Spanish fleet thou canst not see— because
—It is not yet in sight!

And I am tempted to say to those critics who speak of the popular English chronicle play before Shakespeare that they cannot see it because 'it is not yet in sight'. Admittedly, few of the plays acted in the fifteen-eighties have survived. So serious are the losses that the historian of the Elizabethan drama —especially of this period, before the practice of printing plays to be read became popular—often feels himself to be in the position of a man fitting together a jigsaw, most of the pieces of which are missing. Some sort of picture emerges, but is it the true picture? Nevertheless, many play-titles have survived, and a few plays, and if we go by these we are forced into this surprising conclusion: that there is no certain evidence that any popular dramatist before Shakespeare wrote a play based on English history. So far as I know, the only play of this kind for which there is some external evidence that it was written before or in 1588 is *The Famous Victories of Henry the Fifth*, a play of incredible meanness in the form in which it has come down to us, written in bad prose, one imagines, because the compiler could not rise to bad verse. In a jest-book printed years after his death the comedian Richard Tarlton, who died in September 1588, is said to have acted in 'a play of Henry the Fift, wherein the judge was to take a box on the ear'; but when we remember how in every age the snowball of a jester's reputation collects to itself all the jests that lie in its way, we shall not attach much value to this evidence. Other plays like *Jack Straw* and *The Troublesome Reign of King John* and Peele's *Edward I* may well be later than *Henry VI*; and there are no other possible claimants. Again, if we look at the many comments on our popular drama before 1588, most of them made in abuse or defence of the stage, so far as I know we find the same absence of any evidence that the popular play on English history existed before 1588. A writer of 1580 complained that when they wrote histories our dramatists were unfaithful to history, but the themes that he mentions are biblical or classical, the life of Pompey or 'the martial affairs' of Caesar. In 1582 Stephen Gosson, a renegade actor-dramatist, testified from his own experience that the dramatists thoroughly ransacked *The Golden Ass*, *The Æthiopian History*, *Amadis of France*, 'The Round Table', bawdy comedies in Latin, French, Italian, and Spanish, in order to provide plays for the London stage, but the only histories he mentions are *Caesar and Pompey* and 'the Play of the Fabii'; in his unregenerate days Gosson himself wrote a tragedy on Catiline's conspiracy. What a remarkable change of scene when we get to 1592 and can listen to Thomas

Nashe's eloquent praise of plays and especially of plays on English history:

What if I prove plays to be no extreme; but a rare exercise of virtue? . . . for the subject of them (for the most part) it is borrowed out of our English Chronicles, wherein our forefathers' valiant acts (that have lain long buried in rusty brass and worm-eaten books) are revived, and they themselves raised from the grave of oblivion, and brought to plead their aged honours in open presence: than which what can be a sharper reproof to these degenerate effeminate days of ours?

How would it have joyed brave Talbot (the terror of the French) to think that after he had lain two hundred years in his tomb he should triumph again on the stage, and have his bones new embalmed with the tears of ten thousand spectators at least (at several times) who, in the tragedian that represents his person, imagine they behold him fresh bleeding.

My conclusion is, though I am frightened at my own temerity in saying so, that for all we know there were no popular plays on English history before the Armada and that Shakespeare may have been the first to write one.

Suppose this to be so, can we find a reason for it? Academic drama had not fought shy of English history. Thomas Legge, Master of Caius, had written his Latin trilogy *Richardus Tertius*, performed at St. John's in 1579; but academic dramatists had

not to face the censorship of the Master of the
Revels. Popular dramatists, on the other hand,
might have reason to believe, with Raleigh, that
'whosoever, in writing a modern history, shall follow truth too near the heels, it may haply strike out
his teeth'; and in times of national danger censors
might become 'narrow-eyed decipherers' extorting
strange and abstruse meanings out of any subject, however innocent. But when the immediate
danger of a Spanish invasion was averted, and with
this relief domestic broils began once more to be
troublesome, censorship might well be relaxed to
permit a choice of subject that encouraged national
unity. For whatever reason, after the victory of the
Armada dramatists took the risk, and were licensed
to take the risk, of writing plays on English history,
and for some ten years the plays were acted which
have provided many an Englishman with his only
knowledge of medieval history. And as I have said,
for all we know Shakespeare may have been the
first in this English field.

In Dryden's Prologue to his *Troilus and Cressida*
the ghost of Shakespeare is made to say:

> Untaught, unpractis'd, in a barbarous age,
> I found not, but created first the stage.

There is hardly a word here which we should not

wish to modify or contradict. Was that a barbarous age which had already bred a Sidney and a Spenser? Can Shakespeare be said to have created the stage if he followed in the wake of Peele and Lyly and presumably of *The Spanish Tragedy* and *Tamburlaine*? And in what sense was he untaught? Dryden's Ghost continues:

> And, if I drained no Greek or Latin store,
> 'Twas, that my own abundance gave me more.
> On foreign trade I needed not rely,
> Like fruitful Britain, rich without supply.

Here we shall find less to quarrel with. Perhaps Dryden does less than justice to Shakespeare the reader. Shakespeare had some Latin even if his Latin—in comparison with Jonson's—was 'small': it was enough to read in the original some Terence and Plautus, some Ovid and Virgil; and as Dr. Johnson said, he had Latin enough to grammaticize his English, and—we may add—Latin enough to use learned words with confidence and to realize how the marriage of the learned with the familiar enriched his cadences and his meaning. If he read Latin in the spirit of a poet rather than a scholar, even Marlowe's Latinity is not so accurate as might be expected from a Master of Arts of the University of Cambridge, although it is more accurate than those have supposed who have compared his versions of Ovid and Lucan with modern texts rather than with the sixteenth-century texts which he used. Yet though Shakespeare was at some time in his life an avid reader, especially in English books, we may allow that he was less dependent for his nourishment on literary sources than Marlowe. The 'gentle' Shakespeare moved about observing men and manners in court and city, town and country, church and tavern, and the 'ample sovereignty of eye and ear' gave him more than books can give.

'Untaught, unpractis'd.' Shakespeare was of course unpractised until he began to practise. But when did he begin to practise? The first certain reference to him as a dramatist is in Greene's malicious attack of 1592 upon the impudent young actor who had dared to write plays: 'and being an absolute *Johannes fac totum* is in his own conceit the only Shake-scene in a country.' A few months earlier Henslowe's Diary contains a reference to the performance of an unspecified play on Henry VI, and in the autumn of the same year Nashe pays that tribute which I have quoted to the triumph upon the stage of the Talbot scenes in *Henry VI*, Part I. Three references to Shakespeare or his work, then, in 1592, and not a single piece of external evidence to remind us of his existence between this date and the baptism of his twin children in 1585, except a mention of him in 1588 in some litigation of his parents concerning the Arden inheritance. What he was doing during these 'lost years' no one knows. The most attractive tradition and the most respectable—for it comes from the actor Will Beeston, the son of the actor-manager Christopher Beeston who lived in Shakespeare's time—is that he was a schoolmaster in the country. And just so he may have spent some years of his early life teaching himself as well as others the logic and rhetoric which were as necessary to the Elizabethan poet as to the Elizabethan scholar, absorbing too the necessary materials for his invention, in particular the knowledge of Plautus, Seneca, and Ovid revealed in *The Comedy of Errors*, *Titus Andronicus*, and *Venus and Adonis*, and that knowledge and love of the history of his own country which led him to devote to this theme nine out of his first eighteen plays. Shakespeare's was a harder way than Marlowe's, with his six to seven years at the University, but though Marlowe was more learned than Shakespeare, somehow Shakespeare acquired as much of the culture of his age as was necessary to him as a poet.

It is inconceivable that he did not realize that he was to be a poet in earliest youth, yet when we look at the dates which orthodoxy gives to his earliest

work—for example, when we consult Sir Edmund
Chambers, the very pink of orthodoxy and paragon
of caution—we find nothing before 1590-1, the date
to which he assigns *Henry VI*, Parts II and III. Marlowe had written his two plays on *Tamburlaine* by
1587 in which year he was twenty-three, and he was
only two months older than Shakespeare. Did Shakespeare write nothing that has been preserved until
he was twenty-six? The fact is that the chronology
of Shakespeare's earliest plays is so uncertain that
it has no right to harden into an orthodoxy, and
perhaps we should do better to say that by 1592
he had certainly written *Henry VI* (all three parts),
Richard III, The Comedy of Errors, probably *Titus
Andronicus* and possibly *The Taming of the Shrew*,
and that the earliest of these may have been written
as early as 1588.

There are some, however, who are not satisfied
to push back the orthodox dates only one or two
years. They argue that Shakespeare was writing
plays when he was a schoolmaster in the country,
that he began so early that by 1590 or 1591 he had
already reached the maturity of *King John*, to which
orthodoxy assigns the date 1595-7, and that the
author of *The Troublesome Reign of King John*
(printed in 1591) was indebted to Shakespeare's
play in the form in which it has come down to us.

That would not be so much more difficult to believe than the view to which Dr. Hotson would persuade us that Shakespeare had written all his sonnets, mature and immature, by 1589. To the objection that if Shakespeare began to write plays so early it is odd that we do not hear of them before 1592, the answer will be given that he wrote them for country players, and he had to wait until he came to town before attracting the attention of Greene and Nashe. This view has its attractions. All that is wanting is the evidence.

Here perhaps a digression may be permitted on the relation between *The Troublesome Reign* and *King John*. It will reach no conclusion, but it may at least serve to show how criticism is bedevilled by the uncertain chronology of Shakespeare's earliest plays. Capell observed in the introduction to his edition (1768) that certain quartos which we now call 'bad' quartos were either first drafts or mutilated and perhaps surreptitious impressions; 'but whether of the two is not easy to determine'. He committed himself, however, to the view that *The Troublesome Reign* was 'certainly a first draft', and this opinion has held the field with little or no opposition until recent years. He also observed two peculiarities about this play which distinguish it from all the 'bad' quartos of Shakespeare. Although

one play, it was published in two parts with verse
addresses 'To the Gentlemen *Readers*' before each
part; and although the sequence of the scenes is in
substantial agreement with that in *King John*, the
writing is so dissimilar that only two lines (Capell
says only one line) are identical. To quote these
lines is to quote characteristic examples of the kind
of language which these two plays have in common. They are: 'Poitiers and Anjou, these five provinces' (II. i. 528) and 'For that my grandsire was
an Englishman' (v. iv. 42). I see nothing unlikely
or offensive in the orthodox view that *The Troublesome Reign* is a play which Shakespeare rewrote
when he had found his 'new style' about the time
in the mid-fifteen-nineties that he wrote *Richard II*,
and about the time, or perhaps a little earlier, that
he contributed (as many believe) one scene to the
play of *Sir Thomas More*. A young man with his
way to make and the credit of his company to sustain might well employ a part of his time in such
tasks. Yet we still await the *proof* that *The Troublesome Reign* is earlier or later than *King John*:
'whether of the two is not easy to determine', and
such evidence as I have seen seems reversible or
inconclusive. Those who believe that *The Troublesome Reign* is later than *King John*, and an endea-
vour to supply a makeshift play for a rival company

or for a reading public, must explain why it is that a dramatist who remembered so much of the plot and here and there some of the words did not remember any of the language which we think of as characteristically Shakespearian, only colourless matter-of-fact words such as those quoted above. It is not much that we ask for to be convinced that *The Troublesome Reign* derives from *King John*. Just one metaphor of the authentic stamp would suffice, or one collocation of two or three words ordinary enough by themselves yet startlingly beautiful and effective in marriage, or one cadence that can come only from a man with a genius for musical phrasing. A dramatist who is thought to have remembered so much might be expected once or twice to remember so little. But he did not. Perhaps he did not remember them because they were not there. And perhaps they were not there either because the orthodox view is right, as orthodox views sometimes are, or because both *The Troublesome Reign* and *King John* depend upon a lost play, a relationship which some have argued for *The Taming of A Shrew* and *The Taming of The Shrew*. If the latter, then *King John* may be a recasting of one of Shakespeare's earliest productions, traces of which may survive in those passages where *The Troublesome Reign* lifts itself, as it sometimes does, above its usual pedestrian level.

But if we have to believe that our *King John* was written by 1590, then we shall have completely to revise our ideas about Shakespeare's relationship to Marlowe and to other contemporaries, and we shall have to reconcile, if we can, the maturity of so much in *King John* with the immaturity of *Venus and Adonis* and *Lucrece* of 1592–4. No arguments about the difference between dramatic and non-dramatic verse could make that palatable. Very occasionally, it is true, we are puzzled in Shakespeare's earliest plays, by a passage that seems startlingly mature. If challenged to assign a date to the following lines, should we choose an early one or a late?

> O, let the vile world end,
> And the premisèd flames of the Last Day
> Knit earth and heaven together!
> Now let the general trumpet blow his blast,
> Particularities and petty sounds
> To cease! Wast thou ordain'd, dear father,
> To lose thy youth in peace, and to achieve
> The silver livery of advisèd age,
> And, in thy reverence and thy chair-days, thus
> To die in ruffian battle? . . .

It is the beginning of Young Clifford's outburst of grief and anger as he catches sight of his dead father

lying on the field at St. Albans (2 *Henry VI*, v. ii).
'Clearly of later style than the rest', writes Sir
Edmund Chambers, and the internal stopping, the
bold magnificence of cadence and diction, no less
than the strong simplicity of 'Henceforth I will not
have to do with pity', suggest the assured mastery
of Shakespeare's later style. The passage might be
contemporary with *King Lear*. That so good a
man of the theatre would be willing to make petty
revisions in an old play, with all the fussy alterations of players' parts which these would entail, is
unimaginable—the differences between the quarto
and folio texts of *Richard III* have been satisfactorily explained on other grounds—but that the
mature Shakespeare may have been induced to
return to an old play for the purpose of rewriting
an important speech is not contrary to what we
know or may surmise of playhouse conditions. The
case with *King John*, however, is far otherwise. No
rewriting of single speeches, no mere process of
touching up, will account for the steady, subtle
development of the character of the Bastard. Here
is one who begins like a Richard III with an eye to
'commodity' and personal ambition and with something of the same bluff hearty manner of speech;
but here is one who sees the worst, seems to ap-
prove of it, and follows the best. And the ennoble-

ment of the character goes hand in hand with the
ennoblement of the speech.

But I am losing my way, if indeed I have not lost
it, 'among the thorns and dangers' of this specula-
tive world. Before Marlowe's death Shakespeare
had certainly written *Henry VI*, *Richard III*, *The
Comedy of Errors*, and had probably written *The Two
Gentlemen of Verona*, if not *Titus Andronicus*. A rapid
glance over the shoulder at *The Comedy of Errors* may,
perhaps, be allowed for the purpose of reminding ourselves that already in his youth Shakespeare moved in
a world in which Marlowe was not at home and
showed no signs of ever wishing to be at home. The
comedy is middle-class and Plautine and farcical, and
so uncharacteristic of Shakespeare: for the earliest
play that really shows us the shape of Shakespearian
comedy to come is *The Two Gentlemen*. But
already in *The Comedy of Errors* there is the sense
of fun without reference to the correction of manners, the fun of a man who in certain moods finds
the vagaries of human nature and human life a
theme for amused and sympathetic comment. In the
grief of the jealous wife Adriana, which breaks the
bonds of the Plautine convention, there is more
than a hint that to this dramatist comedy is to be
not merely comedy of humours or manners, but
profound comedy, and that women are to play as

prominent a part in it as men. We shall not expect to find, in this middle-class setting, in this whirl of mistaken identity, examples of the conversation of men and women of good breeding, of the exquisite social tact which by nature and nurture was at the command of him who in certain circles is known as the man from Stratford; yet am I being merely fanciful in seeing anticipations of this gracious world of courtesy and civility in such a chance phrase as: 'Sir, I commend you to your own content.' In all this Marlowe has no share. He died before Shakespeare refined comedy and acclimatized it to the public stage, but from the plays which he has left behind him we may doubt whether he could have been successful in high comedy, or whether in low comedy his laughter could ever have been sympathetic. The rain of Shakespeare's genius falls alike upon the just and the unjust, upon the clever and the silly; but if Shakespeare suffered fools gladly, Marlowe did not. And if in his tragedies he is so much concerned with the roguery and stupidity of villainous man, the likelihood is that he would have used comedy for the correction of manners. In short, his comedy might have resembled Jonson's: could it ever have resembled Shakespeare's? But it is hazardous, and also ridiculous, to forecast the development of a genius, and it might be maintained that the tone of *Hero and Leander—suaviter subridens*—reveals a quality which he did not live to express in his plays.

With more assurance we may say that he was never so addicted as Shakespeare to what Quintilian (IX. i. 17) calls figures of speech. We can imagine an E. K. exclaiming at many a passage in *Titus Andronicus* and *Richard III* 'a pretty parison and withal a paronomasia': he would have had fewer opportunities in Marlowe. These two plays are most elaborately wrought. It is as if Shakespeare were writing diploma pieces to show his command of all the artifices of style a poet should possess. R. L. Stevenson called *Richard III* 'a big . . . sprawling melodrama', but while the play is long—one of Shakespeare's longest—it does not sprawl. Every episode, every speech, seems considered, deliberate, and here, as elsewhere in his early plays and poems, Shakespeare dallies with words and word-schemes as if captivated by the shapes into which they may be made to fall. If Marlowe ever went through that stage, it was before *Dido* and before *Tamburlaine* and he has left no record of it. And Shakespeare was soon to work himself free from these 'dulcet diseases', this 'spruce affectation', and to laugh at his own excesses in *Love's Labour's Lost*.

And what of tropes and figures of thought, especially of that trope a command of which, Aristotle has told us, is essential to a poet and cannot be imparted by another? Marlowe is a master of metaphor, but he can do without it. The long speech of Orcanes which I quoted in my second lecture has scarcely an image: the passionate apprehension of the thought is sufficient to kindle the rhythms into poetry. Again, Faustus's leavetaking with the scholars is bare of imagery, yet does not suffer from this bareness. But Shakespeare thinks in images, and his range is already great. He has not yet learnt to use imagery both remote and homely to strike terror to the heart: both 'Heaven's cherubin hors'd Upon the sightless couriers of the air' and Heaven peeping 'through the blanket of the dark, To cry "Hold, Hold"'. It is the later Shakespeare who was to throw the rules of decorum to the winds and prove that imagery, however homely, may consort with the dignity of tragedy if it is vivid and carried to the heart by the rhythm and the musical phrasing. Yet the early Shakespeare has already the power of presenting visual images sharply to the mind's eye. In Barabas's description of his jewels 'Bags of fiery Opals, Sapphires, Amethysts, . . . Beauteous Rubies, sparkling Diamonds', the epithets are conventional, not picture-making, and their success depends upon the associations of the words themselves and, of course, upon rhythm and resonance. But in Clarence's dream (*Richard III*, i. iv. 24) every line, every phrase is a picture, and the speech works up to its climaxes in the changes in the rhythm at the fifth and tenth lines:

Methoughts I saw a thousand fearful wracks,
A thousand men that fishes gnaw'd upon,
Wedges of gold, great anchors, heaps of pearl,
Inestimable stones, unvalued jewels,
All scatt'red in the bottom of the sea;
Some lay in dead men's skulls, and in the holes
Where eyes did once inhabit there were crept,
As 'twere in scorn of eyes, reflecting gems,
That woo'd the slimy bottom of the deep
And mock'd the dead bones that lay scatt'red by.

But I find that Miss Bradbrook has said what I am trying to say when she observes that the picture which Marlowe gives of Tamburlaine's wealth is 'solid enough, but it is not particularised: there are few cases where shape or outline is given to the visual image'.

In any comparison between Marlowe and the early Shakespeare as dramatists there is a danger that Marlowe may suffer by reason of the degradation of his texts. He was, as I have maintained, a man with a vocation for the drama, and no one could have met with his success who had not acquired a sufficient knowledge of stagecraft. It has been maintained that he is inferior to the early Shakespeare in 'the give and take of the dialogue, in which speeches are not merely juxtaposed but articulated', yet the most striking example in our early drama of one speech provoking and determining another is in 1 *Tamburlaine*, where Menaphon's parting line 'And ride in triumph through Persepolis' is caught up by the hero, and we watch it working and fermenting in his mind:

> And ride in triumph through Persepolis!
> Is it not brave to be a King, Techelles?
> Usumcasane and Theridamas,
> Is it not passing brave to be a King,
> And ride in triumph through Persepolis?

But the impression remains that in all that appertains to stagecraft and the technique of the theatre Shakespeare is superior. Critics have taken, and still take, very divergent views of *Tamburlaine*, and if I have defended Marlowe's representation of the character of Edward's Queen, yet it needs defence. And while Marlowe's share in *Doctor Faustus* scales the heights of poetry, the character is revealed to us intermittently in a series of lightning flashes. In the work of the young Shakespeare there

are no important ambiguities, whether of intention
or character. A theme runs through his history
plays and gives each play a unity which it would
not otherwise have, and the chief characters who
embody this theme stand out sharp and clear. And
what a wealth of vivid and consistent character he
can already present, and what a variety! In the
despised 3 *Henry VI* how few are the lay figures,
and how sharply the chief characters are placed
before us: the two kings, Clifford, Warwick, Clarence, Queen Margaret, and, above all, Gloucester.
The scene is almost too crowded. We may wonder
at the strength of that unknown company which had
the honour of giving the first performance, for not
one of these parts may be doubled.

The theme which is so constantly and powerfully
present in his history plays reveals a preoccupation
in which Marlowe has no share. It is even announced in *The Comedy of Errors*, when Luciana
speaks in the following terms to her shrewish
sister:

There's nothing situate under heaven's eye
But hath his bound, in earth, in sea, in sky.
The beasts, the fishes, and the winged fowls
Are their males' subjects and at their controls.
Man, more divine, the master of all these,
Lord of the wide world, and wild watery seas,

Indued with intellectual sense and souls,
Of more pre-eminence than fish and fowls,
Are masters to their females, and their lords:
Then let your will attend on their accords.

We may ignore the special argument of the pre-eminence of man to woman necessary to this particular context—in fact, in Shakespearian comedy it is the women who take precedence over the men—and observe that here is an early statement of the hierarchy of being and the necessity of order. Wherever we turn in the literature of that age we meet with the conception of a divinely appointed order, of a hierarchy of being. A writer on heraldry, John Ferne, observes that there are three hierarchies of blessed spirits, and in each hierarchy three orders; that there is a nobility in natural things also, one in each kind having the pre-eminence: the sun, fire, the cedar, the rose, wheat, gold, the diamond, the dolphin, the eagle, the lion, the king —and the importance to Shakespeare's imagery of these hierarchies needs no stressing; and Ferne goes on to speak of the civil and political nobility, ranging from the emperor to the gentleman; and beneath, the four unnoble divisions of society. But I am labouring a point the importance of which many modern critics have made abundantly clear. Suffice it to say that upon this orthodoxy of belief the early Shakespeare rests and Marlowe does not.

This sense of the importance of order and degree, of the disastrous consequences which follow when they are broken down and civil dissension tears the country apart, this is a theme which runs through all Shakespeare's history plays. It may be more evident in the earlier plays than in the later, because the later concern themselves also with other matters, but it is never wholly absent, and in the early historical plays it is always present. And when this theme is announced, Shakespeare's poetry is eloquent. It is not so with Marlowe. Nor in *Edward II* do we get the same sense that the theme is England and the England of the present reflected in the mirror of the past. More than forty years ago Walter Raleigh observed that the moral which Shakespeare is never tired of repeating is the moral of the chronicler Hall; his English historical plays are written 'so that all men, more clearer than the sun, may apparently perceive that as by discord great things decay and fall to ruin, so the same by concord be revived and created'.

Shakespeare's first four plays were written on comparatively recent history. John Stow tells us that he had himself talked with old men who had remembered Richard III as a 'comely prince', and

in Shakespeare's day as in Hall's the memory of
the wars of Lancaster and York was still vivid in
many an English family whose lineage had been
'infected and plagued with this unnatural division'.
Marlowe's play belongs to a more remote period
in English history, but that does not explain why
these themes never engage his feelings as a poet as
they do Shakespeare's. They are as urgent in
Richard II and *King John* as in *Richard III*: so too
is that sense of the sacredness of kingship and the
inviolable bonds between king and subject, an in-
stinct, Dr. G. M. Trevelyan has said, 'born in every
child of the race . . . wrapped in a thousand mys-
terious associations with a remote and still un-
broken past, transmitted from father to son through
thirty generations'.

If the quotation of one of Shakespeare's many
speeches on this theme be permitted, let it be the
most famous of all, the Bishop of Carlisle's speech
immediately before the deposition of Richard II.

My Lord of Hereford here, whom you call king,
Is a foul traitor to proud Hereford's king;
And if you crown him, let me prophesy,
The blood of English shall manure the ground
And future ages groan for this foul act;
Peace shall go sleep with Turks and infidels,
And in this seat of peace tumultuous wars

Shall kin with kin and kind with kind confound;
Disorder, horror, fear and mutiny
Shall here inhabit, and this land be call'd
The field of Golgotha and dead men's skulls.
O! if you rear this house against this house,
It will the woefullest division prove
That ever fell upon this cursed earth.
Prevent it, resist it, let it not be so,
Lest child, child's children, cry against you 'woe'!

The speech serves to remind us of another advantage Shakespeare has over Marlowe in this kind of play. We think of Shakespeare's history plays individually but we also think of them collectively and their epic sweep. I do not mean that we need to subscribe to the view that Shakespeare planned his plays in two great tetralogies—1 *Henry VI–Richard III* and *Richard II–Henry V*. Certainly, he had decided to write a 3 *Henry VI* before he had finished 2 *Henry VI*, and probably he had decided to write a *Richard III* by the time he had finished 3 *Henry VI*. Similarly, 1 *Henry IV* requires a sequel, though what sort of a sequel I doubt if he knew before he began to write 2 *Henry IV*. And the Epilogue to 2 *Henry IV* promises a *Henry V*, though not the *Henry V* which we are given. Beyond that I should not care to go. But we who have the finished productions before us in the book—and all too seldom upon the stage—cannot but think of the varieties of kingship which he presents and of the links between play and play as the sins of the fathers are visited upon the children. And the Bishop's curse goes echoing down the generations until it is removed at the end of *Richard III* by the establishment of the Tudor dynasty.

I come to an end, but not to a conclusion, and I ask myself which I ought to regret the more: what I have said or what I have left unsaid. In particular I have not been able to speak of Marlowe's poems. They add a new dimension to Marlowe, whereas Shakespeare would still be Shakespeare if all his poems had perished. If it had come down to us without name, who would have thought that that 'smooth song' (as Izaak Walton called it), that type of the Elizabethan pastoral convention 'Come live with me and be my love', belonged to Marlowe? Another example of the truth of Lamb's remark that his works are all of a different kind. And *Hero and Leander*, one of those poems with so strong a forward narrative movement that digression and variety of mood do not impede it, with so much invention and fancy and music that the conceits and rhetorical extravagancies of his time do not fatally injure it. Can as much be said of *Venus and Adonis* and *Lucrece*? Keats told Leigh Hunt that whenever a great poet tells us anything in addition or continuation of an ancient story, he had a right to be regarded as classical authority. Keats has that right, and so has Marlowe by virtue of this poem and of the many passages in his plays in which he breathes the glow of life into ancient myth and story.

If *Hero and Leander* and *Doctor Faustus* both belong to his last year, what a remarkable year! If we could date Shakespeare's sonnet 86 as early as that year, we should be compelled to believe that when he wrote of 'the proud full sail of his great verse', he meant Marlowe. What we may anyhow believe is that in that year there perished at Deptford the only man of Shakespeare's age who could have been a rival poet.

NOTES

(The bold figures at the beginning of each Note refer to pages of the text)

2. W. Pope, *The Life of Seth Ward, Lord Bishop of Salisbury* (1697), p. 111.

5. Stow's *Annals*, augmented by E. Howes, 1615, p. 697 (E. K. Chambers, *Elizabethan Stage*, 1923, ii. 104–5). Howes's statement requires some qualification (Chambers, ii. 105), but is substantially true.

9. For the payments to Peele for the production of Gager's plays, see W. G. Hiscock, *A Christ Church Miscellany* (1946), p. 171, and a forthcoming volume of Malone Society *Collections*, 'Oxford Dramatic Records', edited by R. E. Alton. A record of a payment to Peele of £18 is found in the Vice-Chancellor's Accounts. In the Christ Church Disbursement Book of 1582–3 Peele acknowledges the receipt of £20 from the Treasurer of the College; it seems doubtful if Mr. Hiscock is right in taking this sum to include the £18 paid by the University. Peele no doubt was put to some expense: the payment or payments were not all clear profit. Dr. F. S. Boas unfilially reduces the University's payment to eighteen pence (*University Drama in the Tudor Age*, 1914, p. 180), though Dyce gets it right (*Works of Greene and Peele*, 1861, p. 326).

9. *Thomas Gray*: Norton Nicholls's Reminiscences, *Correspondence*, ed. Toynbee and Whibley (1935), iii. 1290.

10. R. Mulcaster, *Elementary*, 1582, ed. E. T. Campagnac, 1925, pp. 85 and 269.

12. *Pope's distinction*: Spence's *Anecdotes*, ed. Singer, 1820, pp. 24 and 155.

14. William Segar, *Honour Military and Civil*, 1602, bk. 4, p. 228.

15. *Nashe's elegiac verses*. See T. Tanner, *Bibliotheca Britannico-Hibernica* (1748), p. 512.

16. *The date of 'Tamburlaine'*. In a letter of November 1587, first printed in the *Letters of Philip Gawdy*, ed. I. H. Jeayes, 1906, p. 23, Gawdy describes a fatal accident at a performance given by the Admiral's players: 'having a device in their play to tie one of their fellows to a post and so to shoot him to death, having borrowed their calivers one of the players' hands swerved his piece being charged with bullet, missed the fellow he aimed at and killed a child and a woman great with child forthwith, and hurt another man in the head very sore.' In the *Times Literary Supplement*, 28 August 1930, Sir Edmund Chambers correlated this incident with the shooting of the Governor of Babylon in 2 *Tamburlaine*, v. i.

17. See *Gabriel Harvey's Marginalia* (1913), ed. G. C. Moore Smith, especially pp. 54, 109, 144–5, and 157.

18. *Marlowe's first play*. It may well be that *Dido* was written before *Tamburlaine*, but the date of this play and the extent of Nashe's share in it are uncertain. It was printed in 1594 as 'Played by the Children of her Majesty's Chapel. Written by Christopher Marlowe, and Thomas Nashe. Gent.' Its merits are considerable and of a quieter kind than in any other play of his.

20. On Marlowe and Whetstone's *English Mirror* see especially T. C. Izard, *Modern Language Notes*, 1943, lviii. 411–17.

25. Lists of parallels, some of them not necessarily borrowings, are given in Bakeless, i. 205–8 and in R. W. Battenhouse, *Marlowe's 'Tamburlaine'* (Nashville, 1941), pp. 178 ff. The most famous—noted by George Steevens, *Shakespeare* (1793), ix. 90 —is *Tamburlaine*, IV. iii. 119–24—'Like to an almond tree ymounted high . . .' from *The Faerie Queene*, I. vii. 32: here Marlowe has even preserved Spenser's alexandrine. It may be noted that the word 'tender', so alien to Marlowe's genius, appears only twice in these plays—in the scene of Olympia's death (IV. ii. 65), where it is wholly in place, and here (IV. iii. 123). Some of the most striking borrowings are 'epic' similes. No source has been discovered, however, for the long simile at 1 *Tamburlaine*, III. ii. 76–84.

26. The full division into acts and scenes, an uncommon feature in popular plays of this period, suggests editorial revision. Yet more uncommon is the marking of a new scene on the arrival of a new character or set of characters, at 2 *Tamburlaine*, I. v, vi.

33. Swinburne, *The Age of Shakespeare* (1908), pp. 1–2, 4, 14, and *Contemporaries of Shakespeare* (1919), p. 9.

33. *how many of us can boast that we are more than readers?* Many more than when these words were spoken. Tyrone Guthrie's production of *Tamburlaine*, with Donald Wolfit as Tamburlaine, was produced at the Old Vic on 24 September 1951 and ran for five weeks. Some 1,400 lines of Part 1 were presented, and of Part 2 only so much as could be acted in eighty minutes. The audience, therefore, was given a true representation of neither part, but so great was the act of courage in presenting *Tamburlaine* at all that we can hardly censure, though we may regret, the producer's decision 'to lump the two parts together, cut nearly half the text, and serve as one evening's bill'. The effectiveness of the play as spectacle was undeniable. There stand out in the memory: the 'flyting' match between Zabina and Zenocrate enthroned on scaffolds, Bajazeth in his cage and the 'pampered jades of Asia', Tamburlaine's slaughter of his cowardly son, the death of the Governor of Babylon (where arrows were substituted for 'bullets' and without fatal results), and—a brilliant piece of production—Tamburlaine examining the countries of the world, conquered and unconquered, in a map spread out like a carpet and almost co-extensive with the stage. Even more notable was the way in which a crowded audience listened to Marlowe's poetry.

36. *Recent critics*: see especially Helen Gardner, *Modern Language Review*, 1942, xxxvii. 18–24, and G. I. Duthie, *Essays and Studies*, New Series, 1948, pp. 118 ff.

36. *Sesostris*: cf. Jewell, *Defence of the Apology* (1567), p. 422. I find I have been anticipated by R. W. Battenhouse (*Marlowe's 'Tamburlaine'*, Nashville, 1941, p. 169), who referred more appositely to the dumb show before Act I in Gascoigne and Kinwelmersh's *Jocasta*.

38. *the view of life which they present*. For completely opposing views of these plays see R. W. Battenhouse (op. cit.) who sees *Tamburlaine* as a ten-act morality play in which a Christian and orthodox Marlowe presents the downfall of a Machiavellian tyrant, and P. H. Kocher, *Christopher Marlowe, A Study of his Thought, Learning and Character* (Chapel Hill, 1946) who presents Marlowe (in an able exposition) as a highly subjective playwright and a fierce individualist, challenging at every point the orthodox beliefs of his age.

39–40. See L. Hotson, *Death of Christopher Marlowe* (1925), and M. Eccles, *Christopher Marlowe in London* (Harvard, 1934).

40. R. Greene, *Perimedes* (1588), sig. A3.

45. W. Raleigh, *Shakespeare* (1907), pp. 13–14.

47. *every word . . . is dramatic.* Miss Seaton has shown how close Orcanes's lines are to the words of Marlowe's source (Bonfinius, *Rerum Ungaricarum Decades Quatuor*), where Amurath is reported as saying: 'Nunc Christe, si Deus es (ut aiunt, et nos hallucinamur) tuas measque hic iniurias, te quaeso, ulciscere: et his qui sanctum tuum nomen nondum agnovere, violatæ fidei pœnas ostende.' As Miss Seaton observes (*Times Literary Supplement*, 16 June 1921, p. 388): 'Upon Marlowe no longer rests the responsibility of their invention, but merely the responsibility of choice.'

55. '*Who mourns not . . .*': J. Wybarne, *A New Age of Old Names* (1609), p. 81.

57. *Ben Jonson's charge: Discoveries* (Herford and Simpson, viii. 587).

61. *Coleridge: Biographia Literaria*, ch. xv.

65. *The Mirror for Magistrates*, ed. L. Campbell, 1938, p. 371: see also p. 419 and *Parts added to 'The Mirror for Magistrates'*, 1946, p. 252. Thomas Storer, Student of Christ Church, excuses the errata in his verses on *The Life and Death of Thomas Wolsey* (1599, K3ᵛ) with the plea: 'the *Decorum* is kept even in these *Errata*: there is no reason that a book should be without faults, when the person of whom the book entreateth had so many in his life.'

66. Thomas Fuller, *A Pisgah-Sight of Palestine*, 1650, p. 219.

66. Lope de Vega, *Arte nuevo de hazer Comedias*, *Rimas* (1609), Pt. II, p. 206.

67. For the argument that Heywood revised *The Jew*, see A. M. Clark, *Thomas Heywood* (1931), pp. 291–4. Clark would seem to assign to Heywood the 'Bellamira' scenes as well as the 'friar' scenes, on the ground that Bellamira resembles Mistress Mary in *How a Man may choose a good Wife*: but the only resemblance I can see between these two characters is that they both belong to the same profession. L. Kirschbaum (*Modern Language Quarterly*, 1946, vii. 53–56) points out that Aaron's catalogue of his crimes in *Titus Andronicus*, v. i. 124 ff. may have been suggested by Barabas's speech to Ithamore at II. iii. 175 ff., some lines of which I have quoted on p. 63 above, and that in particular the lines

> Oft have I digg'd up dead men from their graves
> And set them upright at their dear friends' door

may have been suggested by the passage in *The Jew*, IV. ii, where the body of the dead friar is propped up outside Barabas's house. Another scrap of evidence, but again not conclusive evidence, that the episode of the strangling of Friar Barnardine may have been in Marlowe's original play is provided by the resemblance between *The Jew*, IV. ii. 16–22 and *The Massacre at Paris*, sc. xix.

68. T. S. Eliot, *The Sacred Wood* (1920), p. 84; *For Lancelot Andrewes* (1928), p. 65.

68. *a . . . play with an invented plot?* In an unpublished essay on 'Marlowe and medieval romance' which I have been privileged to see, Miss Seaton points to the resemblances between the incidents in the last act of *The Jew* and in the romance of *Richard Cœur de Lion* (ed. K. Brunner, ll. 4075–4280). There the Christians are besieging the Saracens. A renegade spy sent out by the Saracens is captured, confesses, and warns the Christians of the mechanism of the town's bridge, a trap with a pit sixty fathom deep beneath. The town surrenders, and is entered with safety. When the captured Saracen amiral plots to murder the Christians asleep after a banquet, the renegade gives warning. As Miss Seaton points out, the incidents do not run exactly parallel. 'But the *points d'appui* of the story are the same: besiegers and besieged; Christians *versus* Saracens, and a *tertium quid*, a spy, a renegade Christian in the romance, a Jew in Marlowe; a mechanical trap with a pit; a false invitation to a banquet.' And if there is no cauldron here, there is one, Miss Seaton observes, in *Beves of Hamtoun* (ed. E. Koelbing, p. 162), where Sir Bevis prepares 'a caudron . . . Ful of pytche and of brymstone', and his enemy is 'cast in the mydwarde'.

69. C. H. Herford, *Studies in the Literary Relations of England and Germany* (1886), p. 251.

70. That Foxe's Book of Martyrs is the possible source of the Bruno episode was pointed out by L. M. Oliver in *Modern Language Notes*, 1945, lx. 391–4.

70. *Marlowe's collaborator*. Nashe and Rowley have been suggested, but inconclusively.

70. See *Marlowe's 'Doctor Faustus' 1604–1616 Parallel Texts*, ed. by W. W. Greg (1950) and *The Tragical History of the Life and Death of Doctor Faustus A Conjectural Reconstruction*, by W. W. Greg (1950).

73. Greg concludes that the scenes and episodes peculiar to the 1616 quarto are 'not late additions, but part of the original, or at any rate of an early, version of the play' (p. 28). The one passage that causes uneasiness is at l. 1200 (IV. i)—'He took his rouse with stoops of Rhenish wine'—which bears so close a resemblance to *Hamlet*, I. iv. 8 (first printed in the bad quarto of 1603): 'The king doth wake to-night and takes his rouse, . . . And, as he drains his draughts of Rhenish down . . . '. 'Rouse' is probably an aphetic form of 'carouse' (*O.E.D.*); no datable example before 1603 is at present known.

77. *Many a preacher of the day*. The two quotations are from Thomas Adams, *England's Sickness* (1615), pp. 86–87.

77. *an English translation*: by Edward Aglionby, *A notable and marvellous Epistle* (1550).

79. *Recent critics*: see L. Kirschbaum, *The Review of English Studies*, 1943, xix. 230–41; W. W. Greg, *The Modern Language Review*, 1946, xli. 97–107; Helen Gardner, *Essays and Studies*, New Series, 1948, pp. 47–53.

82. *as early as 1592 or 1593.* I follow Greg in dating *Doctor Faustus* 1592–3. For the evidence, see his Parallel-Text edition, pp. 1–10. But the evidence is not conclusive, and an earlier date is still possible: see H. Jenkins, *Modern Language Review*, 1951, xlvi. 86.

83. Dr. Percy Simpson (*The Modern Language Review*, 1950, xlv. 509–10) argues that Marlowe pronounced 'Pythagoras' as 'Pythagóras' with the Greek word read according to the accent. He would re-line:

> Ah Pythagóras metempsýchosis:
> Were that true––
> This soul . . .

If we could accept the pronunciation 'Pythagóras', I should not mind re-lining thus:

> Were that true, this soul should fly from me,
> And I be changed unto some brutish beast:
> All beasts are happy, for when they die, . . .

The line 'Were that true, this soul should fly from me', like the next line but one, is metrically deficient, but not rhythmically, for the strong emphases on 'true' (or, if preferred, on 'that') and on 'happy' and the pauses after them compensate for the metrical deficiency. Such a redistribution would be a help to an actor, not a hindrance. Simpson's reading makes a fine sonorous line, but the difficulty is that there is no evidence that anyone pronounced 'Pythagoras' as 'Pythagóras'. The name was firmly anglicized, and the evidence is overwhelming that all Elizabethans, the learned and the not so learned, the Jonsons as well as the Shakespeares, said 'Pythágoras'. See, for example, *The Merchant of Venice*, iv. i. 31, and Jonson (ed. Herford and Simpson), vii. 176 (l. 236) and viii. 61 (l. 2), 88 (l. 156). In the dictionary of proper names at the end of Thomas Cooper's *Thesaurus*, 1584 ed., the accent is marked 'Pythágoras'. If we retain the original lining and the accent 'Pythágoras', we may suppose the actor— in the unlikely event of his bothering his head at all about the metre—to have regarded 'Ah' as extra-metrical, as so often in dramatic verse, and to have slurred the pronunciation of 'Pythag- 'ras metempsych'sis'.

84. John Bunyan, *Grace Abounding*, § 89.

87. *a reported text.* What appears to be a tentative draft of a single episode in the play, possibly in Marlowe's handwriting, exists in a fragment of a single leaf now in the Folger Library. It gives a fuller version of sc. xvi, ll. 1–16, followed by nine lines of verse not represented in the printed text. Once suspected of being one of J. P. Collier's forgeries, it is now accepted as genuine, thanks to J. Q. Adams (*The Library*, 1934, xiv. 447–69) and J. M. Nosworthy (ibid. 1945, xxvi. 158–71). Mr. John Crow kindly refers me to a passage in Thomas Fuller's *Pisgah-Sight of Palestine* (1650), p. 95, which may preserve another scrap of Marlowe's play not found in the mangled printed edition: 'I seasonably remember how one being asked in the *Massacre of Paris*, whether he was a *Catholick* or an *Hugonite*, answered *he was a Physician.*'

87. *De Furoribus Gallicis.* P. H. Kocher has noted that the main source of the first six scenes and of part of the eighth is an English translation of *De Furoribus Gallicis* (1573): *Publications of the Modern Language Association of America*, 1941, lvi. 349–68. He has not been successful in tracing a particular source for the later scenes: *Modern Language Quarterly*, 1947, viii. 151–73, 309–18.

91. The text of the earliest surviving edition of *Edward II* (1594) is unusually correct. There is, however, one curious confusion. In ii. v, iii. ii, and iv. iii, both in speech prefixes and in stage directions, 'Mat.', 'Matr.', or 'Matre.' often appears in error for 'Arun.' (Arundel). (The name 'Matrevis' is nowhere given in full in these scenes.) See the Malone Society edition, p. xii. In the two places in which the error occurs in the text— 'What lord *Matre.* dost thou come alone?' and 'Tell me *Matre.* died he ere thou camst' (iii. ii. 89 and 92)—'Arundel' cannot be substituted for 'Matrevis' without destroying the metre. The error must, therefore, be the dramatist's; and if Dyce is right in attributing it to the doubling of parts by the same actor, Marlowe must be credited with an intimate knowledge of the company for which he was writing.

96. *Machiavelli's maxims*. See Simon Patricke's translation of Gentillet's *De Regno*, 1602, maxims ii. 10 and iii. 9.

101. *A lawn thrust through the throat*. Compare the experiences of Edward Webbe in Naples: 'I was also constrained to drink salt water and quicklime, and then a fine lawn or calico thrust down my throat and pluck'd up again, ready to pluck my heart out of my belly' (*The rare and most wonderful things which Edw. Webbe an Englishman born hath seen*, 1590, sig. D1).

106. *Tarlton's Jests* is in three parts, Court, City, and Country jests. The jest about *Henry V* is in the second part, which was entered in the Stationers' Register on 4 August 1600, twelve years after Tarlton's death. No copy earlier than the edition of 1613 can now be traced, but in 1844 J. O. Halliwell printed from an edition of 1611. Many of these jests are certainly older than Tarlton. One jest in the second part associates Tarlton with Banks's performing horse. The horse had become famous by 1595, but cannot have made its name by 1588 if Jean de Mont-lyard is right. He saw the horse in Paris in 1601–2, when it was 'âgé d'environ douze ans' (tr. of *The Golden Ass*, 1623 ed., p. 250). It should be added that Henry VI, apparently a prisoner in the Tower, presides over *The Seven Deadly Sins*, Part II, the 'plot' or skeleton outline of which has survived. See W. W. Greg's edition of it in *Henslowe Papers* (1907), pp. 129–32. With Lydgate as presenter three sins are acted before the king: Envy (Ferrex and Porrex), Sloth (Sardanapalus), and Lechery (Tereus). The piece has been identified with the second of two pieces written by Tarlton for the Queen's men and prepared for court in 1585, *Five Plays in One* and *Three Plays in One*, the Induction of the former being transferred in the 'plot' to the latter. The 'plot' is, however, of the play prepared for a revival *c.* 1589–92, and we cannot be sure that the play has not been revised.

107. *comments . . . in abuse or defence of the stage*: see the collection in E. K. Chambers, *The Elizabethan Stage* (1923), iv. 184–228

109. '*narrow-eyed decipherers*': *Every Man out of his Humour*, II. vi. 171.

114. *Capell observed.* . . . And before Capell, Johnson had proclaimed his belief that the quartos of 2 and 3 *Henry VI* and *Henry V* were not first drafts of Shakespeare but copies taken down by some auditor during two or three hearings; and the auditor, when he 'had by this method formed something like a play, sent it to the printer' (1765 ed., v. 225).

121. R. L. Stevenson: letter of 19 January 1891 (Swanston ed., 1912, xxv. 51).

123. M. C. Bradbrook, *Themes and Conventions of Elizabethan Tragedy* (1935), p. 139.

124. '*The give and take of the dialogue,* . . .': E. K. Chambers, *Shakespeare* (1930), i. 303.

126. John Ferne, *The Blazon of Gentry* (1586), pp. 5–8.

127. W. Raleigh, *Shakespeare* (1907), p. 41.

127. *John Stow*: see the reference in C. L. Kingsford's edition of the *Survey*, 1908, i, p. xxx.

128. '*this unnatural division*'. Hall, *Chronicle*, 1809 edition, p. 1.

128. G. M. Trevelyan, *England under the Stuarts*, 2nd ed., 1905, p. 232.

130. *Keats told Leigh Hunt* . . .: *The Indicator*, 8 December 1819. He was speaking of Dante's Ulysses. Hunt reveals the identity of his friend in the edition of 1834.

INDEX OF NAMES AND TITLES